Mary Martin's
Needlepoint

1–Frontispiece–*The Family Rug in front of the fireplace in our living room in New York.*

Mary Martin's Needlepoint

by Mary Martin

Photographs by Sol Mednick

William Morrow & Company, Inc. New York

In the theatre I have been unbelievably fortunate to have been directed by Elia Kazan (*One Touch of Venus*), Joshua Logan (*South Pacific*), Jerome Robbins (*Peter Pan*), Vincent Donehue (*Sound of Music*), and Gower Champion (*I Do! I Do!*). With strength, patience and understanding, these men directed me through music, movement and spoken word.

And now my first attempt at putting a book together has been directed by a young woman of integrity and taste, who has been of tremendous practical help. I have been blessed again—this time by the always sensitive, stimulating editor, Narcisse Chamberlain.

Contents

Appendix

List of color pictures

ix

Foreword

One thing I have learned. Never, but never, say you won't do something, because you'll end up doing it every time. At least—among all the other unexpected things that have happened to me during these thirty years of theatre—there are two I had thought surely I wouldn't do.

From the time I was a very little girl to the time my mother made my second child's christening dress, I was aware of expert needlework. My mother could make anything—from a huge, billowing, blue cheesecloth sky that covered the entire ceiling of our school gymnasium for a dance recital, to the most delicate handmade baby dress. I remember having the most exquisite handmade clothes—dresses for all occasions, coats, hats, nightgowns, underwear. And did I appreciate them? Not one little bit! I wanted store-bought clothes.

And those seemingly endless fittings! I can still hear my mother saying, "Mary, if you would just stand still for five minutes!" I promised myself I would never wear anything handmade again so that I would never have to have another fitting. And I told myself I didn't want to learn, couldn't learn, to sew—anything.

And so, I ended up spending three to four hours a day, three to four times a week, for as many as six weeks in a row, standing for fittings to get every costume perfect for each show. And then I took up needlepoint. I had to take it all back—I did want to learn to make something, to do something quiet and untheatrical and all my own in off-stage hours.

Wouldn't you say there is justice somewhere in this for

my blessed mother? And who brought about that justice? My husband, Richard, one day in 1950 when he brought The Rug backstage to my dressing room at the Majestic Theatre when I was appearing as Nellie Forbush in *South Pacific*. A whole front-hall rug, that is how I started.

This book will tell you only how to begin to do needlepoint. Richard dared to coax me into it because he had been told it was easy, and he had been told correctly. Needlepoint works, almost right away, for real beginners. Just as quickly, it becomes more personal and more interesting than the mere stitching of it. That is why this book is almost all about why I did each exciting new project, and for whom—especially for whom. As the saying goes, "If I had to do it all over again," I would do it *all* over again, because it has been fun, stimulating, quieting, and full of moments of meditation, of thinking.

My words of wisdom for anyone who wants to take up needlepoint are, "Jump right in. Don't be afraid to try anything. Anything—even a front-hall rug. If your husband doesn't understand and doesn't bring one home to you, he'll understand later. Go out and get it yourself!"

Have fun, looking, reading, and stitching,
My love,

Mary Martin

Mary Martin's
Needlepoint

The Rug

The Rug is known by a variety of names. It was the innocent, impulsive beginning—all five and a half by seven and a half feet of it!—of my doing needlepoint.

First, it was The Hall Rug. For months, Richard and I had been shopping unsuccessfully for a rug to put in the entrance hall of our new country house in Connecticut. Discouraged, I finally exclaimed, "I'll bet we could *make* one better and cheaper than anything we've seen!"

Unwary words! Richard took me up on them immediately. For one thing, playing Nellie Forbush in *South Pacific* at the time, I was learning that I needed to spend my off-stage hours not idle, but quietly hoarding my strength; Nellie was a very vital, energetic girl and it took a tremendous amount of *my* energy to keep her that way. And then, Richard had heard a thousand times how my mother enjoyed doing needlework of all kinds and how I now wished I were not so hopelessly untalented in this respect. He had also *heard* that needlepoint was very easy and an absorbing and restful pastime. He didn't really know the first thing about it, so he was taking a very long chance that Sunday afternoon when I proposed we should actually make a rug. He said it should be a needlepoint rug, and we spent the whole evening talking about the design and the colors.

All the details were to have something to do with the family and the Connecticut house. Already, it had acquired its second and most lasting name, The Family Rug. In his famous needlepoint shop on Madison Avenue, Robert Mazaltov greeted our ideas with infectious enthusiasm and worked out the over-all design on canvas for us exactly as we had visualized it.

October, 1950, a Saturday—the rug canvas was ready to be picked up at a perfect time. Heller, our daughter, had been in bed with flu and was at the restless period of convalescence. I would be home all day the next day. Both of us would stitch on it, and with great excitement we would see the rug take shape, it would be ready in a few days, or weeks, or maybe a month or so . . .

When Richard stopped to pick up the canvas and wool, Mr. Mazaltov managed to pry out of him that no one in the family had ever done needlepoint before. Considering the complexity of this project, he was surprised, not to say apprehensive. He insisted on showing Richard how the stitches were to be taken, explaining that one certainly did not "merely push a needle in one hole and out the next" as we had assumed.

•..

Richard, Heller with one of the poodles, and me, in Connecticut at a very early stage of The Rug.

WALLACE LITVIN

The actual stitching began the next day, Sunday. Richard stood between Heller, in her bed, and me, in a chair close by. We started. "I think that's what he said to do," said Richard, unconvincingly. "But look, Heller's doing it differently and hers looks better." I think maybe it did. This was a day of trial and error, putting in and taking out. The rug had been made in two separate panels. I insisted on starting with the petit-point design of the house in summer. It didn't occur to me to look for something easier. Heller started filling in background on the second panel. We had accomplished little by the end of the day, but we were optimistic that we would finish within two, not more than three months. . .

I kept one half at home and the other half in my dressing room at the theatre. Dear Gladys Hardwick (her initials are at the lower right-hand corner with Heller's and mine, along with the dates, 1950–51–2), Gladys was my maid at the theatre and she frequently picked up the panel to fill in background around the petit-point designs. By Eastertime, the panels were getting heavier, and I took one to Bermuda on a week's vacation. I took it to the beach and stitched away in the sun and then by the warm fire at night. After I had played in *South Pacific* for over two years, Richard and I took a motor sailor along the East Coast and the still-unfinished rug went with us. I stitched on deck, in the cabin during rain storms, and it went ashore with us for a week end on Cape Cod. By now it was The Traveling Rug, and its travels had only begun.

I was to open in *South Pacific* at the Theatre Royal-Drury Lane in London that fall. We decided to leave early and take the children, Heller, aged seven, and Larry, aged seventeen, on a motor trip from the northernmost counties of Ireland down through the central and southern portions. I needle-pointed my way in and out of dozens of the inns and hotels of Ireland—and of Scotland and England, too—before we reached London where we arranged to settle for two years. The children, the rug, Richard, and I stayed at the Hotel Savoy briefly until we found our flat at Grosvenor Square.

Richard, The Rug, and me on a short vacation in Bermuda.
The Rug is getting heavier, but we have a long way to go.

All of us (including the rug) spent one of those heavenly, long English week ends with Noel Coward at his home near the white cliffs of Dover. We (including the rug) had Sunday suppers at his house in London. Noel had long since become very familiar with the rug. I didn't spare him the sight of it again in England. And I took it on flying trips with Richard to Paris, Rome, and Taormina, Sicily. In Taormina, we found an antique door frame with a design of gilded ivy leaves. The owner didn't want to part with it, but we persuaded him we had to have it by showing him the ivy design on the rug we intended to use by the door.

Weeks, months, we had said . . . it was almost two and one half years. Excitement in the family grew when we finally could see that now it was only a matter of days, weeks

5

If there is righteousness in the heart there will be beauty in the character. If there be beauty in the character, there will be harmony in the family home. If there is harmony in the home, there will be order in the nation. When there is order in the nation, there will be peace in the world.

The Chinese proverb on The Family Rug.

at the most, before I took the very last green stitch of the border. The last day, I worked the whole day, thinking that at any moment I would finish, but still I had to take the rug with me to the theatre. There I did, I did at last take the very last stitches. And that was the night that Noel Coward came backstage before the curtain went up to tell me Princess Margaret was in the audience and that he would bring her backstage after the performance.

Princess Margaret had launched ships, she had walked on royal red carpets, but tonight she would have a welcome with a difference! During intermission, I arranged the champagne and glasses; after the final curtain, I rushed to the dressing room and carefully laid the rug in front of the door sill. We, The Rug and I, were ready. The door was swung open by Noel. Princess Margaret was about to enter when Noel looked down and said in his glorious, clipped, *audible* English voice, "Oh, no!—Not that bloody rug again!"

Back in Connecticut, at long last we had a family ceremony as we placed the rug in our own front hall. There, we had been able to enjoy it barely a week when I was invited to send it to a needlepoint exhibition in New Hope, Pennsylvania. Before it was returned, a notice and a ribbon came announcing it had won first prize. The Prize Rug. Noel had a name for it, but we had still another. Many letters followed (one week, there were ten) asking me to send it to cities as far away as Detroit, Philadelphia, Pittsburgh, and Boston. Some asked for it for needlepoint exhibitions, others

6

for charity organizations, asking permission to charge admission just to look at it! For almost two years, it was away from home, longer than it ever rested on our hall floor.

It had its greatest triumph on Edward R. Murrow's "Person to Person" television program, on April 30th, 1954. During our televised visit, he asked me specifically about the Chinese proverb that is stitched in the upper right-hand corner. This Richard had found when we were doing research before I started rehearsals as the faithful wife in *Lute Song* in 1944. Some scholars credit Confucius as the original author, others say the author is unknown. As the TV camera showed a close-up, Ed Murrow asked me to read the words aloud . . .

> *If there is righteousness in*
> *the heart there will be beauty*
> *in the character. If there be*
> *beauty in the character,*
> *there will be harmony in the*
> *family home. If there is*
> *harmony in the home, there*
> *will be order in the nation.*
> *When there is order in the*
> *nation, there will be peace in*
> *the world.*

The next day, Ed called to say that telegrams by the hundreds requesting copies of the proverb had poured into his office and that the CBS switchboard was jammed with calls making the same request. Two days later, they had received seven thousand letters in the mail asking for copies and, the following day, when it was estimated that twice that many were delivered, it was agreed that all the secretaries at CBS, and more, couldn't take care of this big and pleasant surprise. Quickly a folder was made up showing the rug on the front, with the proverb printed inside. As the years go by, the proverb seems more apt than ever.

Certainly I hesitate to advise a beginner to start in on needlepoint with a rug five and a half by seven and a half feet with—I think—eighty-four separate petit-point designs and five six-foot ivy vines on it. However, since I didn't know any better, it turned out to be a fine way to begin, for I have never been much afraid of trying any needlepoint idea I have had since. So far, I have never done anything this big again though, because once I got started so many more ideas came to me that I turned to smaller projects just to try to keep up with them.

There is one thing I very much do advise, however. Do some petit point on your very first canvas. You should know right from the beginning, from your own experience, that petit point is no more difficult than the larger needlepoint, only slower, and that the finer stitch makes all sorts of design ideas possible that simply will not work in a large stitch. Petit point is only a matter of "splitting the mesh" of what is called double canvas, while using exactly the same stitch as you do for needlepoint (this is explained on page 128). And, as a beginner, you should conquer double-mesh canvas right off, anyway. Single-mesh canvas is a little easier to work on, but the difference is so slight, you will make things much easier for yourself in the long run by beginning on double mesh and throwing in a bit of petit point for good measure (which you cannot do on single mesh; see page 128 again). I would suggest making your first canvas something small on double canvas, and then switching to a fast single canvas for your first big project—perhaps your first rug?

Here is how we planned The Family Rug. The over-all design is reminiscent, in a primitive way, of a romantic French style of design. The five lines of ivy represent our favorite green-leaf plant for growing both inside and outside our house. The lines of rosebuds at either side and the roses and rosebuds placed at intervals in the five main columns represent the very old plantings of pink and red climbing roses that grew over the ancient stone walls surrounding our property in Norwalk, Connecticut. The background is a soft

8

green-grey, the plain border, tones of harmonizing green. The chief accenting colors of the petit-point designs are shades of rose and red and green. That was the basic plan, into which we so enjoyed injecting to suit ourselves our own family motifs and symbols.

The first column begins with a rooster head, one of a pair of handsome red, French ceramic roosters four feet high, given to us by Jean Arthur, which stood on the stone entrance posts of the driveway. The cat was Heller's and, three flowers further on, a sprig of cherries and leaves represent the first tree she dared climb by herself. The grey miniature poodle was Heller's, too. And the clasped hands are a very important symbol to us.

The second column shows our house in winter, then Heller in a costume she wore at the age of five when she made her stage debut, playing the part of the youngest sister with me in *Annie Get Your Gun*. The comedy-tragedy masks represent the theatre, the apple is for our espalier fruit trees.

The third column has hyacinths, my favorite spring flower, the beige miniature poodle that came to keep the grey one company, the house in summer, and a bouquet of flowers Heller sent to me once when I was seriously ill. The column ends with the second ceramic rooster.

The last column has the Chinese proverb. Next is a golden wheat field with a rose and a guitar. This was a special place of my son Larry's imagining when he was a boy—a place where he wanted most to be when he played his guitar and sang. Next, among the roses, are strawberries that we loved to pick before breakfast to eat with heavy cream. And finally, the loveliest elm tree we know, which stood on our land in Connecticut. Previous owners and natives nearby used to argue whether it was the second or third oldest elm in the state. It mattered very little to us—it was ageless and always beautiful and for a little while it was ours.

And that is what the rug is about—the family and the house. There could be, I think, just such a rug waiting to happen in any family, about any home.

10

Winter and summer, the living room

About twelve years ago, The Family Rug left the country with us and came to New York. There it has led a less hectic, traveled, prize-winning, televised life than it did in its early years and seems content to be The Hearthside Rug in our living room, where you see it in the Frontispiece. We have been content to let my commitments in the theatre keep us here, too, for two and three year stretches, winter and summer. This is home and it is important to us. The rug is where it should be, between the two small sofas on either side of the fireplace—the comfortable spot we use by far the most and where, indeed, I do a great deal of needlepoint.

We are frequently asked, "How can you have your needlepoint rug in a place you use so much?" Or, "Why don't you hang it on the wall?" It never occurred to us to use the rug anywhere but in a place where we could see it and enjoy it constantly. It has never been protected (it has been used in a front hall!), and it does not show any sign of wear and tear. As for hanging it like a display on the wall! Although my blood boils at the idea, I try to be tactful and say calmly, "Oh? I hadn't thought of that." I have seldom been understanding or sympathetic when I have seen needlepoint used as a showpiece on a wall, and especially not needlepoint in a frame. Most needlepoint pieces are fun to make, designed originally to be used as pillows, upholstery, or rugs, and meant to be just as serviceable as they are decorative. Certainly there are exceptions. Pieces designed specifically to be framed or used as wall hangings would be equally impracti-

2–Pillows for summer,
the "geranium" design.

3 & 4–On the following
pages, a corner of the
living room in winter and
the same corner in summer.

cal and out of place as chair seats or on the floor. But if
needlepoint is designed to be used, it should be used.

The color scheme in our living room in winter begins with
the rosy beige of the paneled walls, the fabrics are beige
and yellow-gold, greens, accents of rose-red. On one of the
two small green velvet couches at either side of the needlepoint rug are needlepoint pillows I did long ago—two of
bright cyclamen rose with flowers of strong yellow and a
small olive-green flowered one between them. In the evening
the gold silk curtains are drawn, all the colors and textures
are rich and warm, winter colors, welcoming as the fire in
the English fire-urn on the coldest days.

We love this version of the living room, but I can hardly
wait when the first signs of spring come to see the same
room, within the same walls, become another room, ready
for the hot summer. Now the same couch and all the couches
and chairs are covered with a Fortuny striped cotton of rose
and gold and beige. The doors onto the terrace open wide,
and we can see the United Nations building and far down
the East River. On the terrace, we successfully keep a variety
of geraniums with blossoms of white, pink, coral, and red,
but inside we rarely have flowers during summer—they wilt
so soon—but keep instead many kinds of leafy cool green
plants. All the rugs are taken away to be cleaned—The
Family Rug to be washed—and we enjoy having only the
bare polished-wood floor. Everything is simpler—cooler.

But, flowers belong to summer. Over the years I have
made a good supply of flowered needlepoint pillows that
could give this touch of color, but they seem so woolly and
hot that most of them have ended up in slipcovers of the
same striped cotton that covers the furniture. Several years
ago, I was trying to finish a needlepoint pillow during an
early heat wave. My hands were moist, the wool was hot,

2

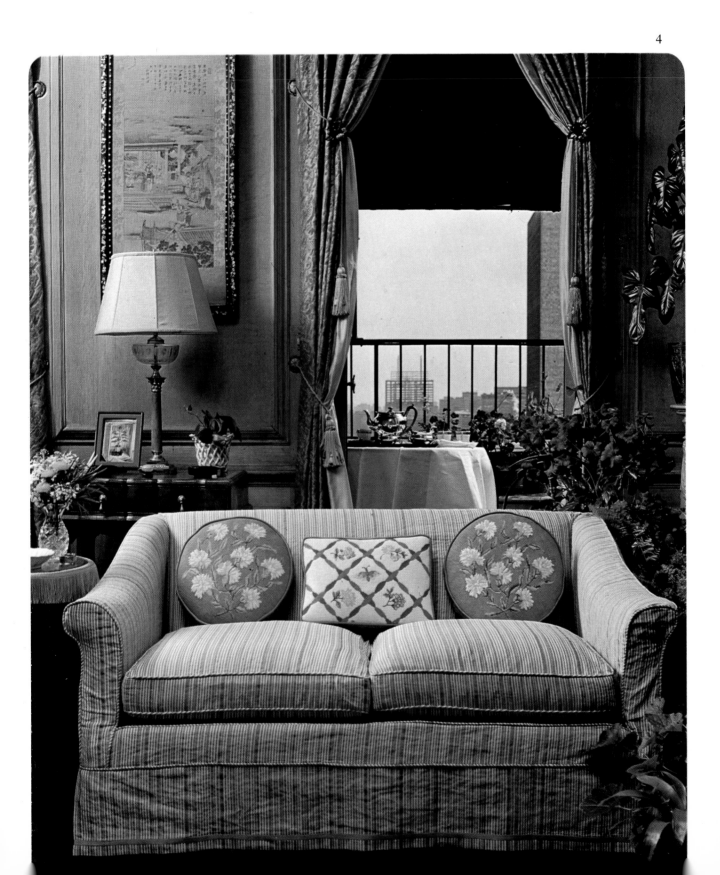

5

6

*5 & 6–The Hands, actual
size (page 15), and below a
collection of hands
(page 20).*

I was enduring this needlepoint instead of enjoying it. I remember I had been thinking with satisfaction that all the winter clothes had been gotten out of the house to be dry cleaned, that the freshly laundered slipcovers and a supply of summer clothes had been ready in time for the early weather, when the idea struck. Of course, it should be the same for needlepoint! Cool, washable, summer cotton needlepoint—with flowers.

From a sample card of many colors of English cotton embroidery floss, I chose bright leafy greens and colors for flowers that I might like to have as fresh flowers in the summer living room. Yellow carnations—they remind me of a memorable sight, the acres and acres of carnations we never tired of looking at in front of the home of Captain Edward Molyneux, the designer, when we visited him on the French Riviera, at Biot in the area near Grasse where flowers for French perfumes are grown. Enthusiastically, I made a pair of .yellow and green cotton carnation pillows. Then, roses against an ivory background, in a design I liked as soon as I saw it because of the diagonal ribbons in colors that pick up those of the slipcover cotton.

At the opposite end of the living room is a long slipcovered couch with many covered pillows and two cotton needlepoint pillows with large geranium designs. Yes, those are geraniums, though they look more like some kind of undersea flowering coral bush. The rather curious colors imbedded in the brilliant green background work so well with the cotton-stripe colors that I don't worry at not having captured those geraniums very well. I have seen many geranium designs and experimented with designs of my own, and this one flower I do find difficult and I have assigned a future date to try it again.

Meanwhile, the summer living room is cool and fresh and it has "flowers." The warm wools and velvets and silks are banished—and then, to tell the truth, with the first brisk days of late September, I can hardly wait to have the winter living room back again.

Cotton needlepoint is a delight to work. The thread feels remarkably like silk, and it does not have the drawback of fraying as silk sometimes does. I have been warned that it will probably not wear as many years as wool will, but I don't care and it certainly feels very sturdy.

The cotton pillows in the summer living room were done on twelve-stitch-to-the-inch canvas (see page 131), which I tested in advance to be sure that the English embroidery floss would cover it well. You must not pull your stitches too tight; cotton does not "bounce back" in the stitch quite the way wool does. The English cotton I have used comes in glorious colors, some of them more vivid than I have seen in wool, it has an exceptionally silky texture and good body. I used it because I had become familiar with it in London, and the best brands are available in this country. But there are other embroidery flosses available that will work well, too. (Do not, by the way, confuse embroidery floss, which is a loose strand of many fine cotton threads, with mercerized embroidery "thread," which is much finer and firmly twisted.)

Be sure to buy plenty of it (it comes in very small skeins), especially of the background color, for, later, if you buy additional cotton of the same color but of a different dye lot, you may end up with a slight but very perceptible shift in the background coloring; it will show up as a definite diagonal line in the background basketweave stitching (page 138). This is, by the way, something to remember whether you are using wool, silk, or cotton; be sure to get enough of the background color at the beginning. The dye lots of good needlepoint wool are the least likely to vary.

The
Hands

I started The Hands (color picture 5) with the greatest excitement. We were still in London, where I had long since discovered the Royal School of Needlework—a place where one always feels a warm welcome. On one of my periodic visits, Miss Ward showed me a ragged piece of the finest canvas I had ever seen. She assured me that it was the smallest mesh they had ever had and that no more would be available.

Way back in my mind, I had long planned that one day, when I knew more about needlework, I would do Richard's and my clasped hands "free hand." I had heard that some very experienced, very professional, most daring needlepoint enthusiasts refused to stitch on anything but a blank canvas. Incredible and impossible, I was sure, and stitching on this incredibly fine mesh seemed impossible, too, but all my instincts urged me to try, for a special reason.

Clasped hands had always been important to me, as they were to every young Texas girl, as a symbol of friendship. It was Richard who made of them our own family symbol by giving me the most beautiful clasped-hands friendship ring I had ever seen—on a Saturday night, in Hollywood, twenty-nine years ago. I had never met anyone from whom I really wanted to receive such a ring before, which explains what happened next. Within moments the friendship ring became an engagement ring and only hours later it was our wedding ring when we eloped to Las Vegas. This wasn't quite as Hollywood as it sounds, as we phoned Richard's mother in New York and stopped at my mother's house on our way out of Los Angeles to tell her and my son, Larry. What was rather Hollywood was that we had to drive back on Sunday so I could start making my second motion picture at 6 A.M. on Monday!

Since then we have discovered carvings, bibelots, artifacts of all kinds in the form of hands and clasped hands. Dear friends have given us many unusual ones, and complete strangers, people who have heard of our interest, have sent hands to us with heart-warming messages. I have used clasped hands in many needlepoint designs, but these tiny petit-point hands are my own most dedicated contribution to the collection, made especially for Richard. We usually keep them on a particular table in his study for reasons that I will explain.

That day in London—it was in 1952—I rushed back to our flat with the scrap of canvas, grabbed the family sewing box, and searched for the silk thread I had seen somewhere in there a few months before. It was wisp-thin and soft, in several lovely shades of beige, made for darning real silk stockings, long, long ago. I don't know how the silk had found its way into my sewing box, but there it was, and I was about to start on a new adventure.

I selected the darkest flesh-beige tone of silk, threaded the needle, picked up the canvas, took a deep breath, and began with Richard's thumb. There was not a sound in the apartment from any direction. Richard hadn't returned from his appointment, Heller was still at the Royal Ballet School, and the cook had not started preparing our early dinner. I was not conscious of the stillness as I changed the shade of silk several times and the stitches slowly formed the thumb as I had visualized it. I was never able to duplicate those moments of total absorption during the remainder of our stay in London, but I knew that I could look forward to our return home soon by freighter, our favorite way to travel. Then there would be hours and hours on deck with the sun pouring down, giving me the perfect light to see how each stitch slowly formed what I hoped eventually would represent our clasped hands.

There were only three passengers on the freighter, Heller, Richard, and myself. We were astonished when we went to our cabins, after staying on deck for over an hour watching the ship get under way, to find all our suitcases unpacked, our things neatly put away in the chests of drawers, dresses and suits hanging in the closets. We were still marveling when a handsome couple entered, introduced themselves, "James and Agnes Harvey," and announced that tea was ready in the salon. James added, "If you'll be good enough to give us your trunk keys, we will unpack while you are having tea." Before the end of the day, we learned we were traveling with the head steward and stewardess of the Queen Mary. This was their way of spending their vacation—or, "Our eighteenth anniversary," Agnes said.

I remember little else except their thoughtful service, days and nights of quiet, the calm seas and sunny skies, and sitting for hours in the sun concentrating on the tiny canvas with the silk threads. I was oblivious to everything, the family had to inform me two and three times each day that lunch had been announced. Reluctantly, I occasionally had to leave the hands that were slowly beginning to take shape as I had dared hope they might. We touched North Africa—very colorful, but something aboard ship was more colorful. We pulled up at two ports in Spain. Oh, yes, very colorful and very exciting. But it was more exciting to get back to the ship to finish Richard's fourth finger and to progress, perhaps, on that gloriously clear day to the white cuff at my wrist.

On leaving Spain, we were not to see land again until we reached Cuba. There were more of the same cloudless days, sea air, and brilliant sun. I worked for hours with my chair turned so that the sun poured over my left shoulder onto the canvas. Then I found that sometimes I could see better by holding it in the shade. Gradually, it seemed I accomplished more when I wore dark glasses. Heller said I frowned a great deal of the time and Richard claimed my eyes were growing smaller. Finally, when I wouldn't even stop long enough for tea, he declared, "I've heard about compulsive drinkers, but a compulsive needlepointer is something new!"

The days continued clear and strangely rewarding, but soon there were not many left and I seemed to accomplish less. The sunlight dazzled my eyes. The always observant Agnes brought cotton pads and a bottle of witch hazel. "You've been rubbing your eyes a great deal lately, Madam, perhaps these will cool them. Why not lie down a while and let me . . ." I succumbed to her ministration, but with my eyes refreshed, back I went on deck to complete Richard's dark suit cuff. Only two more days, and I was anxious to finish before we reached Cuba. I managed, but just barely, for I lost the power of concentration as we approached land. I was too excited—at seeing Cuba again after eleven years and, more important, the Leland Haywards had cabled that they would meet us at the dock. Nancy had been the first friend to give me expert needlepoint advice. I couldn't wait to show her the finished clasped hands.

Up with the sunrise on landing day, one last quick look at the small canvas, and then the rush to get ready. As I brushed my teeth, I looked up into the mirror. To my amazement, I could see only one eye—the other was solid, startling red. It was only a burst blood vessel that was quickly attended to, but tropical sunlight and petit point were not the ideal combination I had thought. What a funny, one-eyed sight I was when the Haywards greeted us!

I really hadn't the slightest idea how we would use this piece of work. Richard was definite. "It must be framed." That would be fine, but I was rather diffident when he insisted we take it to the House of Heydenryk in New York. Mr. Heydenryk is one of the world's most expert framers and a man of great judgment and taste.

He took one look at the canvas and exclaimed, "I knew it! I knew it! Twelve years ago, I knew it!" As he tried to open the bottom drawer of his desk, he repeated, "I knew it. Now if I can only get this drawer open." With another yank, the drawer, stuffed with a mass of papers, bits and pieces and odds and ends fell to the floor. "When I saw the frame, I knew I must have it, I knew one day someone would bring me the very picture that belonged in it." He pushed papers out right and left. "It's down here. I've kept it hidden, but it is here . . ." He finally found the hidden treasure—a tiny hand-carved gold frame made in Italy in the seventeenth century. "See!" he announced. "See! They belong together. Leave me now. Leave me. I have another idea. You will see. Thank you for giving me this pleasure."

When the package arrived several weeks later, we couldn't have been more surprised to see that he had dared to put the tiny canvas in the perfect small frame against a comparatively bold, modern walnut panel. It *was* perfect. Mr. Heydenryk knew of the two tiny gold oval plaques, portraits of me done by my friend Electra Wagner when I was in *South Pacific*, and had phoned to ask Richard if he might borrow them. There they were, enchanting details, returned indeed, and exactly where they belonged.

At some time or other, all of us make conjectures about a rather fascinating hypothetical situation—which of our possessions would be the most important to us to save in case of fire? Not long ago, we were talking about this with friends, but it was a much more poignant conversation than usual, for recently their home had actually burned to the ground. In turn, each of us named something we might choose above all else to rescue. When we came to Richard, he did not hesitate. "I'd take our clasped hands that Mary did."

He is a very satisfactory husband.

. . . .

The extraordinarily fine canvas on which the clasped hands were done is very scarce—presumably, and not surprisingly, because it is not much in demand! It is sometimes called "gauze" and is usually made of silk. If you ever see any, you will understand why I worked on it free hand, without having the hands drawn on it. Though a design could, of course, be indicated on the gauze, it would have to be done in the form of very light guide lines, as any heavy markings would obscure the already hard-to-see mesh. By all means, a clear drawing on paper of what you want to do is a great help for reference if you work free hand.

....

Just a few of the hands in our collection are shown in color picture 6 with Richard's petit-point hands, arranged on the antique Chinese altar table in his study. Above them hangs the photograph Horst took of me at the time I sang "My Heart Belongs to Daddy." Richard never ceases to be amused by the contrast between the sentimental clasped hands and that leggy photograph. On either side are the black-and-white Wedgwood urns that were presented to us at the luncheon the Wedgwoods gave for us at their factory when we were in England, the same year I did the hands. In front of the hands' frame, on the right, is a tiny ivory figure of a Japanese woman washing her hair, a gift, when I was "Wash(ing) That Man Right Outa My Hair," from the owner of Cameo Corner in London. To her right is the gold cigarette lighter Heller and I gave Richard in 1947 while we were in Chicago and Heller was playing my "baby sister" in *Annie Get Your Gun*.

The ivory clasped hands on the left were brought back to us from Paris by the fabulous woman who had played baby-sitter to my son Larry many times when I first went to Hollywood—Hedda Hopper.

It was from Rome that the Leland Haywards brought us the handsome antique clasped hands made of steel edged with gold set with tiny diamonds and rubies. There is a button to push at either end which opens each cuff. Some way this was for a lady to keep perfume, others have told us this is where she kept poison!

The two hands at the far left are among the gifts from dear people, strangers we have never met, who simply sent them with their good wishes.

The handsome, large black hand was a most unexpected

gift from two gentlemen, Cy Feuer and Ernie Martin. They are Broadway producers who, among other hits, produced *Guys and Dolls*, *Charlie's Aunt*, and *How to Succeed in Business Without Really Trying*. We had met and talked for more than a year about a new show they wanted to produce especially for me. They even flew to the farm in Brazil with the composer and lyricist, where we talked, listened to music, and I became more and more interested, and then excited. I had really committed myself to that show when suddenly I changed my mind. I have never really approved of invoking that supposed privilege of women and/or actresses. But I *had* changed my mind, and I told them, and we parted friends.

Some months later, as I was about to leave for the theatre on the opening night of *I Do, I Do!*, a box was delivered. I took out this handsome Siamese hand and read the note wishing me "Every happiness on this exciting night for us," signed Cy Feuer and Ernie Martin. On a New York opening night, a friend is a friend in need and a friend indeed. I performed that evening knowing there were friends in the audience, among them two understanding gentlemen who had already added very much to my happiness.

Richard's Wall

The petit-point clasped hands have been on many tables in many rooms, but they belong to Richard and we like them best on the antique Chinese altar table against what is called "Richard's Wall." The pictures that hang there represent a career to which Richard's support has been indispensable. In a sense, the tiny framed canvas of our clasped hands is the support for everything on the wall.

When Gertrude Stein says "a rose is a rose is a rose," I am not quite clear on what she is saying until I change the word to one that has a more specific meaning for me. "A home is a home is a home!" And one of the best ways to make a home a home, when there is an actress in the family, is *not* to have one photograph, one portrait, one drawing of that actress anywhere in the house! However, as you can plainly see, I have had to compromise. Richard does not entirely disagree with me, but the moment came when he demanded as his right the freedom to do as chose with at least one wall he could call his own.

Richard's Wall, as he pointed out and as the whole house could hear, is in his room, his study, and it is the wall to your back as you enter. "If you don't want to see it," he exclaimed, "walk out of the room backwards, or keep your eyes closed!" I know Richard likes his wall and I have to agree it is of interest to us both. Besides which, it looks very well in this particular room where the color scheme is black and white, beige and red.

That kindly man, that deft artist, Al Hirschfeld, of course,

is very much responsible for the success of the whole. He has drawn me for *The New York Times* since *One Touch of Venus* and for each opening Richard has arranged to buy the original drawing. Somehow Al Hirschfeld always captures the spirit as well as the humor of the part I am playing. The remainder of the pictures are Richard's favorite photographs of me in various parts.

At the top left, you see Peter Pan flying joyfully over the head of Captain Hook (Cyril Ritchard). Next to it is our favorite photo taken by *Look* Magazine during a performance of *Peter Pan*. Next, to the right, is Maria in *The Sound of Music*, in her rich, nunlike wedding gown designed by Mainbocher, photographed by Toni Frissell. And then to the far right, Hirschfeld showing Maria with Captain von Trapp (Theodore Bikel) and all his children in *The Sound of Music*.

In the middle row at the left, Hirschfeld shows Nellie Forbush dancing merrily in her Honey Bun sailor suit to the open arms of Emile De Becque (Ezio Pinza). The large center Hirschfeld drawing is of the moment when Agnes protested she would *not* go to pot as Michael (Robert Preston) had predicted when he boasted that "It's a Well Known Fact" that as men grow older, the more attractive they become! And next is Hirschfeld's Venus, singing "I'm a Stranger Here Myself" to Sono Osato, Kenny Baker, John Boles, and Paula Lawrence.

At the left of the bottom row is a miracle photograph by Philippe Halsman of Nellie in the huge Honey Bun sailor suit. It was truly a miracle that probably only Halsman could have accomplished. Early on the day we were to leave for New Haven to give a first performance of *South Pacific*, *Life* phoned asking that I spare the time to have Philippe take a cover photograph for the magazine. This was one of the first concrete signs that, out of the air, people sensed the show would be as big a hit as we had hoped and prayed.

The invitation from *Life*'s editors had a special meaning for me. They had taken their first photo of me for a cover when I sang "My Heart Belongs to Daddy." While we were

24

trying out *One Touch of Venus*, they had photographed me again (at 4 A.M., after a rehearsal!) and later ran four pages of style photos of Mainbocher's exquisite costumes. In still another issue, they had published a faithful and lengthy biography of me.

This time, however, I had a problem. I had fallen asleep in the sun. Never had my face been so burned, and now it was at the worst possible peeling stage. I could not imagine anyone wanting to photograph such a sight nor how anything could be done about it. But they kept asking, then urging, and then insisting. There was nothing left for me to do; these men were my friends, I could only explain to them by showing them my white-flaked and scarlet face.

I walked reluctantly into Halsman's studio. He looked at me and said, "Yes, yes, yes," and turned towards a chest of drawers. "Yes, yes, yes." He reached into a drawer, took the lid off a large jar and, between another "yes" and another, he gently patted my cheeks with cold cream. He said "yes" again and smiled, spreading the cream over forehead, ears, mouth, chin, still repeating, "Yes, yes." He seemed very pleased. He stepped back to look. "Yes. Get into your costume and we are ready. This will work! It will! You will see."

When I had changed, he patted my face again with soft tissue paper, then added more cream, and again pat, pat with the paper. Now he had me stand under the hot glare of the studio lights while he peered through the camera. Then, "Get to work! Do your stuff! Yes, yes, yes," and I sang and danced Honey Bun many times that early afternoon while Philippe clicked his shutter. He smiled. He beamed. And finally, "Yes," once more, and I was convinced that this time he really meant he was delighted. He had tried to perform a miracle and it worked. *Life* used the picture on its cover and was the first to hail the coming to New York of the smash hit called *South Pacific*.

There were perhaps more photographs taken of me the year I sang "My Heart Belongs to Daddy" than had been taken in all the years before. One was outstanding, taken by

In another corner of Richard's study are two challenging examples of needlepoint, neither of which I did. The pillow in the wing chair and the valance around the edge of the draped table we found at different times in different parts of England. They are of the same Victorian "school" in design and coloring—and they are both heavily beaded. They are here to be enjoyed but also to remind me that I have much to learn. I want to do needlepoint with beads! I have made a few feeble tries, but I look forward to a time when I can really begin under the guidance of an expert, for I have many ideas, many plans for my "Beaded Needlepoint Period" in the future.

the kindly, talented, sensitive Horst. I am grateful that we have the only copy, the picture centered in the bottom row on Richard's Wall. There she is, "Dolly Winslow," who thirty years ago started everything that has happened since.

Last, and definitely not least, on the far right is the swirling figure of Venus, in heavenly sheer pink chiffon designed by Mainbocher. She was captured one hot, exciting afternoon by Gjon Mili in his studio on Fourteenth Street. That long session was simply fun for me. I did not realize until later what a suspenseful day it was for the vital, personable Mili. This was the first time he had deliberately used for an assignment the lightning-fast strobe lights with which he had been experimenting. He took many pictures of me in many different costumes that afternoon, as I walked and ran and sang and danced back and forth the length of his big studio. He seemed pleased, we were both exhausted by sunset. We shared another jubilant moment some months later when *Vogue* printed between two and three dozen of his photos, a triumphant proof of the success of all his hours and years of perfecting this action-camera technique.

On the extreme left of the table is the porcelain figure by Keating Donahoe of the faithful wife I played in *Lute Song,* and on the far right a figure of Peter Pan. And finally, in the very center, are the petit-point hands. The canvas is so very small—really tiny—with the high wall, the large photos and drawings above it. But we see the clasped hands there, very clearly. Richard says it is they that make it a meaningful wall.

7–The painting at the right, of a bowl of blue hydrangeas, is by Janet Gaynor, who gave it to us as a housewarming present for our house in Brazil. But we bring it with us to New York to put in the glass sunroom of the apartment along with the needlepoint pillows and rug it inspired.

8 & 9–The rug and the two hanging panels on the following pages were made for the sitting room of Vossa Casa, the guest house at the farm in Brazil (page 33).

Flowers for the farm in Brazil

I love to paint, too. Although I have yet to finish a painting that looks anything like my original concept, I am very serious when I paint. "Delightfully primitive," "terribly amusing," say family and friends, trying to be polite and encouraging, not realizing I don't want to be primitive or amusing.

I think often of our very dear friend Janet Gaynor when I paint, for she really is an artist. I have caught glimpses of her at work—a tiny, feminine figure in a becoming smock, every hair on her head in place, she looks like an adorable portrait-miniature of a painter. Then she picks up a brush that always seems much too large and vigorously starts to mix colors. After a brief pause, she begins and seemingly never stops. In the stillness of her studio, you can yourself feel the vitality, energy, and strength that pours through her brushes onto the canvas. Invariably, the final results are exciting, especially her paintings of flowers. Artists and critics no less than her friends praise her work. Nevertheless, the paintings soon disappear, put away to be seen no more.

I know of only two exceptions. One was done not too long ago when Janet came to visit us in Brazil. The view from a

particular spot in front of our house interested her. There, through the lacy tops of a long, low line of yellow and white margarettes, you can see a sweep of rolling hills beyond. She painted the picture and left it hanging near one of the doors that leads to the same view, without saying anything about it.

The other exception is an earlier picture and was even more of a surprise. After months and months of delay, we were actually moving into the house in Brazil, "Our Farm" Nossa Fazenda. It was small and still unfinished, but work had been done we had not yet seen. We rushed excitedly in and out, exclaiming over discoveries and surprises, behaving much like the farm chickens which had been thrown into cackling confusion by our arrival.

And then we were still. The chorus of chickens and voices outside seemed to fade. On the wall in front of us was a painting, our favorite of all Janet's paintings, a bowl of blue hydrangeas.

I had happened to see Janet painting these hydrangeas of many shades of blue while we were staying at her home, Fazenda Amazonia. I say "happened," because Janet never announces anything, except perhaps that lunch or dinner is served; she begins a new painting and finishes it without fanfare or comment. Unless you are right there and very much on your toes, you would never know a picture had been started, finished, and put away. Janet weaves the threads of living with a light, delicate touch, and the hydrangeas I had so much admired preceded us to Nossa Fazenda without our knowing anything about it.

We were settling in a remote part of a country which was new to us, there were enormous quantities of practical matters to attend to, and we gave little thought to frills and decorations. The first room that had to be made livable was the bedroom. We started with a bed, a kerosene lamp, a table, a chair, and Janet's painting.

The painting is still there whenever we are and, in time, with no apparent effort, things simply gravitated to that room that were sympathetic to the blue hydrangeas on the white wall. By accident, coincidence, whatever it was, we stumbled over pieces of hand-carved wood—all that was left of the first church built by the Portuguese in the State of

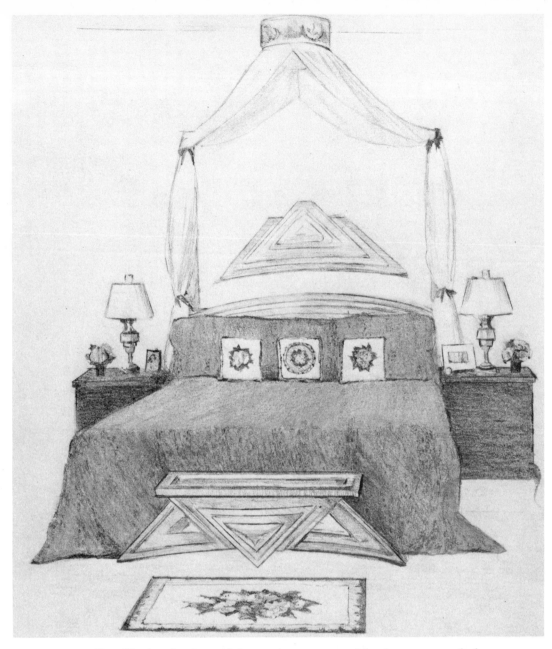

Brasilia in the late eighteenth century. My heart pounded with excitement when I saw the original paint on the wood, Janet's hydrangea blue! We bought all there was, loaded the jeep and raced home. The drawing shows what we were able to fashion of this beautiful wood. The headboard, the two wall pieces that just show at either side of the white net curtains, and the bench seat at the foot of the bed are all made of it. There was another handsome portion which we put over a doorway. Pieces of the wood have the lovely original blue, others that were slightly touched by the sun are paler, while others that the sun struck more directly are still paler. But all of them are shades of Janet's hydrangeas. The crown that holds the net curtains at the top is made of beaded needlepoint we found in England. It is full of hydrangea blues. And there is a blue rug, made of cotton we grow on the farm. The spinning, dyeing, and weaving were all done on the farm.

Naturally, needlepoint inspired by the hydrangea painting was bound to happen. So far there are three pillows and a small rug. I would still like to do another version of the rug so there would be one for each side of the bed. In the meantime, the painting, the rug, and the pillows have two homes, as we do. They travel frequently with us from Brazil to New York, where they fit in the scheme of our small glass sunroom (color pictures 7 and 10) as well as they do in the bedroom at Nossa Fazenda. And as I write this, Nena Smith—who has looked after my costumes on Broadway and on tour, packing and unpacking trunks and suitcases from Alaska to Texas and around the world—is finishing a duplicate of the hydrangea rug. Of all the pieces she has seen me work on, it is her favorite. Nena, Mrs. Kirby Smith, has done it for her home in Palm Springs, California, not far from where the original artist, Janet, now lives.

The design of the hydrangea rug is stylized and by no means a copy of the painting. The border is a repeat pattern I had used once before (color picture 18). The background is a bisque color I never would have thought of without seeing it first in the painting.

The hydrangea painting, and the natural flowers, too, ranges in the color spectrum from yellow-green to violet, with somewhere in between the one special shade we refer to as "Janet's blue." I knew it would be a wonderful sequence of colors to work with. I had the hydrangea designs painted for me on the needlepoint canvases; that was a job beyond this "primitive" and "amusing" painter. For the circle on one pillow and the edges of the rug, the "leaf" border was used that Richard had designed for me for the violet pillow in silk petit point which I had been working on for years (page 130 and page 132). The rug is worked on the usual ten-stitch-to-the-inch rug canvas, the pillows are twelve stitches to the inch. (This proved not to be fine enough to do the best rendition of the small leaf repeat pattern in the pillow circle; if I had only used a double instead of a single canvas, I could have split the mesh and done the circle in petit point.)

We referred directly to the painting in choosing the wool colors, and working with them *was* a joy. The adapted hydrangea designs are much more appropriate for needlepoint than any attempt at copying the painting. But using a painting as a color guide is very rewarding. You cannot follow it literally, but it leads to a better choice of yarns and tells more about possibilities for shading than can be painted on the needlepoint canvas. The canvas design is only a limited version of what the design could become as to color. You find yourself taking liberties with the canvas, doing better than what is indicated on it. You begin to get the feel of "painting" with the wool. This is really something to try, and I don't hesitate to recommend that beginners try it, for you are always perfectly safe following what is on the canvas if the variations you try to borrow from the painting become too much for you.

Some years ago, we returned to New York after an especially rewarding stay in Brazil during which we had watched the workmen on the farm finish our new guest house, Vossa Casa ("Your House"). It was late fall, but the cold gray days were more like mid-winter, the threatening skies for over a week had been promising snow.

I had worked on so many pieces of needlepoint at Nossa Fazenda that I needed skeins of yarn of various colors to finish them. So one bitterly cold afternoon, I headed for Mazaltov's again, on my way to a voice lesson. I was halfway there when the snow came, lovely light flurries fluttering down. In a few moments it was dark as early evening, within minutes the streets and sidewalks, the automobiles and hurrying pedestrians were white with snow. You could not see in any direction, cars stopped, horns blew, people ran, bumping into one another. By the time I reached Mazaltov's, the street lights had come on and all the shop windows were lit. I stood on the sidewalk dazzled by the lights shimmering through the huge white flakes. And then, beyond, clearly I saw the sunny green-and-white rug, with its huge bold flowers in tropical shades of shocking pink, orange and yellow, lavender and deep purple. It almost leaped out at me from the shining window of Mr. Mazaltov's shop, and I felt as though I were looking into the sunlit white sitting room of Vossa Casa.

The sitting room had worked out the size and shape we had wanted, all white as we had wanted—white ceiling, walls of white tile, a sweep of white curtain, white wicker furniture. It was cool and pleasant, but so far it had no character. It needed a theme, a centerpiece to pull it together—the very thing that appeared in front of me that afternoon, thousands of miles away in a blizzard in New York.

Because everything at the farm is very simple, I think the needlepoint we have used there has been more important to each room it lives in than any I have done. This rug (color picture 8) was only the beginning of the Vossa Casa sitting room. Several months went by before I realized that it would stand alone like an unrelated island of colors unless we let it lead us to other things. That was when I had the same design adapted for the pair of wall panels, the "tapestries" (color picture 9) that have proven so versatile and useful. As it turned out, they were finished before the rug. We hung them first on either side of a wide mirror that faces the window wall of the room. They are just the length of the mirror and with a table below they looked well there. But now we like them better hung at either side of the wide window on the opposite wall, where they can be seen a second time reflected in the mirror. The couch, covered with plain green material that matches the green borders of the needlepoint, sits under the window piled with quantities of silk pillows of all the brilliant colors of the needlepoint flowers, and the rug lies on the dark-yellow floor in front of the couch. The deep seat cushions of the wicker chairs are covered with the same green material as the couch, and each chair has a bright silk pillow to tuck comfortably into the small of your back.

34

We indulged in one more accent, a round coffee table covered with a dramatic floor-length circle of shocking-pink silk. We couldn't resist that silk which we had seen billowing in the breeze outside a shop in our nearest little Brazilian town of Anapolis one day. In fact, there were two different shades of shimmering shocking pink, both brilliant, each trying to out-do the other, and equal yardage of both was used in making the table cover.

What I love the most about Vossa Casa is not in the sitting room at all but outside the wide window. There stands a grove of tall trees, part of the original jungle, and at eye level as you look out you see a collection of orchid plants in hanging baskets and attached to the tree trunks. The flowers are yellow and white, lavender and purple, like the flowers in the tapestries. The view is at its loveliest when the very high and gracefully long yellow ballet orchids are in full bloom, the lavender and deep purple ones blooming at the same time, a rich note of color against the brilliant sunlight that filters through the foliage.

This is quite a sophisticated room to find in central Brazil, but it is somehow right in its tropical setting, so different from the moment in the snow that inspired it. It is one of those rare rooms that does indeed adapt itself to every type of weather, cool and refreshing on the hottest day, cheerful and comfortable no matter how hard rain beats against the window. It seems to please our Brazilian friends the most of any room at Nossa Fazenda.

It will, I hope, be a long time before I again begin such a big project as this rug and the pair of tapestries. They are done on rug canvas, ten stitches to the inch, which is fast to work on, but still, they did take a long time. However, one of the joys of needlepoint is that when a piece is finished, all the moments of doubt when the task seemed so endless are forgotten and only the pleasure of its having turned out well remains. If another idea came along that promised to grow as successfully into a whole colorful room as the flowers for Vossa Casa did, I would probably launch forth recklessly into an even larger rug this very day.

....

A detail of design worth pointing out about this rug and its two "matching" tapestries is that though the colors do match, the design in the tapestries is a very free adaptation (and the two of them are not even quite identical), a long vinelike version of the loose bouquet on the rug. The flowers, leaves, everything is smaller on the smaller panels than on the rug. I think we would never have enjoyed these pieces together so much any other way; if we ever planned a second trio like this, we would want some appropriate difference between rug and panels again.

A practical point, when the wall panels are blocked and mounted, ask that the backing material for them be very sturdy, or the tapestries will not hang straight and flat as they should.

Heller's first needlepoint

In 1945 and 1946, we were in London while I performed at the Theatre Royal-Drury Lane in Noel Coward's *Pacific 1860*. Even though the war was over, wherever you looked, sights and sounds reminded you of the destruction and suffering the people of this island had endured. Food was none too plentiful and shops of every kind were sparsely stocked.

Nevertheless, one bright, sunny afternoon Richard, Heller, and I found our way to The Trading Post which, we had heard, had recently received a shipment of assorted goods. Still, when we arrived, at first we saw mostly empty tables and shelves—until we saw, all three of us, a long yardage of English linen floating down from a high shelf. The colors, the design, the feel and fresh fragrance of the linen delighted us at once. We had not the slightest idea where we would use it, but we were so overcome with our discovery that when the clerk asked us how many yards we would need, we decided to take the entire bolt.

At home in Connecticut, our living room had three exposures that looked out onto lawn and trees and flowers as far as the eye could see. When we got back, we knew immediately where to use the English linen; with its vines and birds and flowers, it was ideal for full-length curtains to frame our country view. For summer, all the furniture was slipcovered in the same material. It was one of the happiest, most comfortable rooms we have ever lived in.

It was for this same house that we started The Rug in 1950, which became too awkward and heavy for Heller to help me with. She was only eight, but it was she who thought to ask if she could do a pillow of the bird and butterfly, flowers and leaves adapted from the linen (color picture 11). She started with enormous enthusiasm; she took great pride in having her very own piece of needlepoint to do. The time came, though, when several weeks and then several months would pass before Heller seemed able to remember where she had put her needlepoint last. Of course, I should have realized that the petit-point portions would be tedious for a healthy eight-year-old. Naturally she enjoyed climbing trees, ice skating, and playing with her schoolmates more than relaxing sedately with her needlepoint.

Some years later, I found the unfinished piece in a doll's trunk and I finished it. But there for all of us to remember were all the stitches Heller had done on her first needlepoint, even to the change in the shade of wool she had used in the beige background. The linen has since moved on with us to several different homes. It is as new and fresh as the day we first saw it in the store and now, over twenty years later, the last of it covers the walls of the guest room in our New York apartment, where we show off Heller's pillow as proudly as ever.

The needlepoint bug had struck Heller more than we knew. In the years to come, we were to see her constantly starting or finishing or planning one piece after the next. I insist she inherited this interest from me. I envy a little that she also inherited from my mother a talent for the finest sewing, comparable to what the most accomplished professionals can do.

The very sentimental rocker

When I was a new-born baby in Weatherford, Texas, this was the rocking chair my mother used when she held me in her arms and fed me. That is the sentimental beginning to its sentimental story—which I think is just as it should be.

The first time I was aware of the rocker, the wood was a dark reddish brown, the worn upholstery a print of faded lavender. Eventually, the rocker came to me. We had recently bleached the handsome antique cradle that awaited the birth of our daughter, and we bleached the rocking chair to match the cradle. I had pink and white curtains at the windows of the nursery and my mother quilted what was left of the material with an ivy-leaf design to reupholster the chair. We were convinced, of course, that Heller would be a girl.

Twenty years later, it was Heller who was preparing a nursery, for her first baby. But pink . . . or blue . . . she was not as certain as we had been whether she was carrying a girl or a boy. There was only one other possible color, yellow when in doubt? She had bought a number of charming Mexican plaques, silhouettes of circus animals in pink and blue and yellow, to hang as a frieze on the longest wall. The room was soon painted a sunny yellow and progress was being made. But Heller felt an urgency to finish the room, so I went over one afternoon to look at it once more and help decide how it should be arranged.

The cradle Heller had used was ready. The worn little

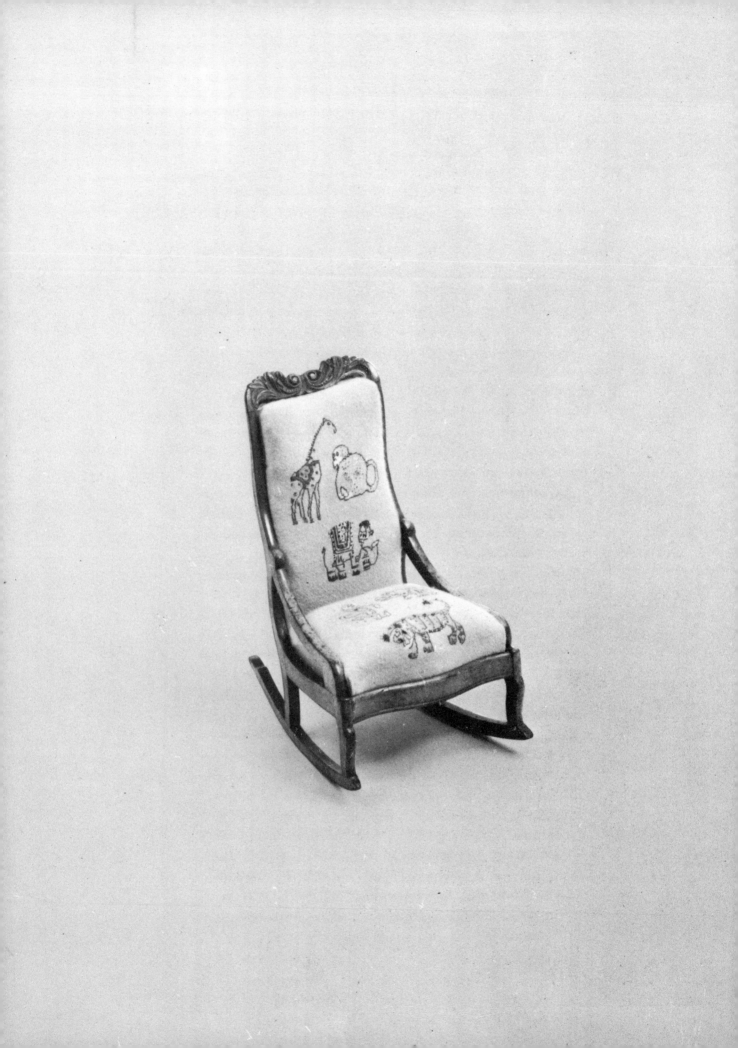

rocker stood alone at the other end of the room. The animals were waiting, propped up on the floor—the giraffe, the monkey, the elephant, the lion, the rhinoceros, and the bear. Heller and I both adored those animals, and I remember looking at our smiling daughter and knowing we had both thought of the same thing. There we suddenly were, trying to arrange the animals on the faded upholstery of the rocker. Moments later, with our arms full of wooden animals, we were rushing to Mazaltov's to pick out needlepoint wools to match.

The following days and nights, whether Heller and I were separated by the twenty city blocks between our homes, or together visiting, or I was at the theatre between performances, we were both stitching away at a headlong pace. There was a date to meet. The doctor had even said the baby might arrive on one of three specific days. Heller stitched the seat of the chair while I did the back. This was unlike any needlepoint project I had ever done. It was for my mother's rocking chair, for my rocking chair, for our daughter's and her baby's chair. It HAD to be finished by a certain day, one of the most important days in a woman's life. It was not the relaxing experience I was accustomed to with needlepoint and the lovely excitement reached a day of almost ridiculous celebration when both Heller and I had finished our pieces. We washed, stretched, and dried them, and then we clambered into a taxicab with the chair and sat on the edge of our seats all the way to the upholsterer's.

He was most understanding and as he looked at Heller he assured us repeatedly that he would put aside less pressing jobs in order to deliver the chair in time for the homecoming.

I have repeatedly been told I am sentimental. This I do not deny, though what is sentimental and what is realistic appear to be very much the same to me. I only know what I see and hear—like the sight of Heller bringing home her first baby, Timothy; walking with him in her arms into his bright, sunny room; carefully sitting down in the family rocking chair; and smiling. I was smiling, too. At the same time there were tears in my eyes—so perhaps it is true— I am sentimental. And I'm glad.

....

If you are having your finished needlepoint mounted by a needlepoint shop, you can safely leave the blocking to be done for you. But if an upholsterer is to mount it, he may or may not have workmen who are accustomed to this. It is really very easy to block any relatively small piece of needlepoint yourself (not anything big like a rug; that is too much). All you need to do is keep a paper pattern of the original size and shape you want the pillow or upholstery or whatever to be; it will get out of shape as you work on it. When the piece is done, trace or tape the pattern onto a board. Wash the needlepoint, pat, do not wring, out the excess water, and tack the needlepoint into place on the pattern. This takes some pulling and hauling; don't worry, needlepoint can take almost anything (except tacks that are not rustproof; be *sure* they are rustproof). It is best to tack the center points of all four sides into place, then work out from the centers to the corners.

The family coat of arms

What to give one's parents for birthdays and Christmas is never an easy decision to make, in any circumstances, and traveling parents such as we make it no easier. Early in 1965, Richard and I realized we would be in London for Christmas, for I had returned to the Theatre Royal-Drury Lane to appear in *Hello, Dolly!* We would be thousands of miles away from Heller and her family, the customs would complicate an exchange of presents even more, and we made an agreement, *we* thought, to celebrate Christmas when we came home, late in 1966.

•..

11–Our daughter Heller started this pillow when she was only eight. It was her first piece of needlepoint, and it was her own idea to have the design adapted from the English linen in the background (page 37).

Therefore, we were very much surprised to receive a box from our daughter a few days before Christmas. We were enormously proud and pleased, and quite emotional, when we unwrapped the package on the day itself. It seemed incredible to us that Heller was aware of the Halliday coat of arms. Only once had we used it, for about a year, on a small quantity of stationery. We did very much like the design itself and especially we agreed with the motto, which means "To Be Rather Than to Seem to Be." Heller was no more than five, perhaps six at the most, the year we had used the crest. Now, once again, as parents we were amazed at what appeals to the young, what they remember.

Later, we learned that early in the summer Heller had gone to the engraver, the same one we have always used, to ask for the die, and she had found the time to needlepoint the design, in beiges, black, and burnt orange, colors which she knew belonged in our library in New York. She added the modern Halliday symbol—the clasped hands. Great waves of affection and appreciation swept over us that Christmas day of 1965! And more than ever, because it was made by our own daughter, we understood the pleasure of receiving a piece of needlepoint—and I remembered, too, for the thousandth time that, for all the other pleasures of doing needlepoint, not one compares with the pleasure of giving it away.

....

The coat of arms is one of the very few pieces of needlepoint we have ever used framed. The formal design, the symmetry of it, make it right to display like a print or a drawing. It is surprising how seldom this works with needlepoint designs. Needlepoint is most often decorative in the same sense that a very rich fabric is decorative and usually works best used as a sort of fabric—for hangings, upholstery, pillows, rugs, almost anything but a formal picture. But this was an exception, and a very good one, too.

11

12

13

12, 13, & 14–On the preceding pages: bottom left, in Richard Rodgers' study, petit-point sketch of Dick's hands writing the music for "Bali Ha'i" for South Pacific; top left, in Oscar Hammerstein's study, petit-point sketch of Oscar writing the lyrics of "I'm in Love with a Wonderful Guy" for South

Pacific; and right, Leland Hayward, producer of South Pacific, and his wife, Nancy, on the telephone, in petit-point.

15–Opposite, for Joshua Logan, director of South Pacific, needlepoint and petit-point stage set, photographed in his living room.

South Pacific

There are things that happen, things that people do for you—there is nothing you could possibly do to repay them, to say thank-you enough. You cannot even try, at least not in a literal way. The four *South Pacific* pillows were gifts, very small gifts, to four people who made that show great and in the process made something of Mary Martin that she had not been before. It is not the needlepoint pillows that matter, but my thoughts as I worked on them, the hours of "visiting" I had with Richard Rodgers, Oscar Hammerstein, Joshua Logan, and Leland Hayward, as I stitched quietly by myself and remembered everything they and their wives, Dorothy and Dorothy, Nedda and Nancy, had meant for so many years both to me and to Richard. These are some of the memories I stitched into the four little pillows . . .

To begin almost at the end, there was the night I gave my last performance in New York as Nellie Forbush before we went to London. About half way through the last act that night, firemen and policemen from all around the Broadway theatre district started coming into the Majestic, standing at the back of the theatre. And then people from other theatre box offices, newspaper columnists, photographers, and taxi-cab drivers came. Ours was the last curtain to go down—between 11:25 and 11:28—and gradually actors from other shows, some still in make-up, and their dressers, and even stagehands and ushers from the nearby theatres crowded in,

45

pushing the earlier arrivals down the aisles until there were solidly packed columns of people right down to the orchestra pit.

As Emile and Nellie touched hands and the curtain started down, the sound of all those thousands of voices filled the theatre and the music played and played and the curtain kept going up and down and up again. And then, unlike what had happened at any other performance, four SeeBees in fatigues, with their backs to me and the packed theatre, slowly came onstage carrying a long metal pipe with one of the big mechanical props we had used—a part of an airplane engine—dangling in the middle. They reached center stage and turned around—and there were Dick, and Oscar, and Josh, and Leland! Oh! How I remember! More music and shouting and whistling and the next thing I knew, somehow a black velvet box has been gotten out of the prop and put in my hands. Someone had to help me open it. All the lights were lowered except the spots which were all turned blindingly on me as I slowly lifted from the velvet box a glittering, shimmering bracelet of gold and pearls and diamonds . . .

Heller was still awake when we got home and we showed her the bracelet before we went to get ready for bed. All was quiet until much later, when, out of the dark we heard Heller calling, "Mother! Mother! Do you realize there are fifty-two pearls and sixty-four diamonds in this bracelet? ! !" Oh, the unnerving, unabashed, wonderful directness of children!

And there was a sequel to this story, for at the end of my twelve-month appearance in *South Pacific* in London, the very same four gentlemen placed on my finger the gold and pearl and diamond ring which they had had Schlumberger design to match the bracelet.

The first three *South Pacific* pillows are my own way of doing "portraits." I never have been able to do faces well in needlepoint, nor even when I paint, but I can do hands, which are especially meaningful to me. And so, the beige and white, brown and black portrait of Dick Rodgers is really of his hands as he wrote down the notes of "Bali Ha'i" without even going to the piano to play them first (color picture 13). The pillow today is in the little beige and brown study Dorothy Rodgers decorated for him. Seeing it photographed there reminds me again of how Dorothy always finds the right place for everything. Whatever she touches happens easily and beautifully. It was pure pleasure to appear at a benefit Dorothy organized for charity, it all went off so exactly on schedule, apparently with the greatest of ease. And then, in completely different circumstances, she and Dick were such real friends to us once when Richard was very ill. But perhaps I thought most often as I worked on this pillow of how I never tire of seeing Dick standing before an orchestra, conducting; he has a strength, a simplicity, a sensitivity at such moments that is memorable. And I remembered the first time Dick played "I'm in Love with a Wonderful Guy." He played it once and a second time and without stopping started the third time. I was so excited I joined in and sang at the top of my voice and fell off the piano stool on the last high note. As he leaned over to help me up he said, "Never sing it any other way."

Once in a while as I stitched, Richard and I listened to recordings of music, going way back, that Dick wrote with Larry Hart and then with Oscar Hammerstein. With Oscar! Oscar wove through all the years of my professional life practically from the beginning. I was straight from Texas and still in my teens when I first auditioned for that great and dear man. I knew that was what he was the moment I saw him, but I had no idea he was already one of America's great lyricists. He loved to tell the story of that audition. When he asked what I was going to sing, I said in all innocence, "Oh, a song you probably haven't heard of, 'Indian Love Call,' "—a song which he had written, of course, with Sigmund Romberg! I really don't blame Richard for finding it difficult to understand how Oscar could see anything in me way back then, but he did, and he took the time to arrange many more auditions for me and kept track of my progress, and that was all long before I met Richard.

Later, much later, Oscar and Dick asked me to make a decision. We were in Hollywood and Vinton Freedley, who had produced the show in which I sang "My Heart Belongs to Daddy," wanted me to return to New York to star in *Dancing in the Streets*. But Dick and Oscar had also talked to us about my going back for their show, *Green Grow the Lilacs*. They phoned from New York—Richard and I were in the middle of lunch at the Brown Derby—and they wanted to know if I had made up my mind. They were starting to write the very next day and wanted to know before they began. I just couldn't think. I asked Richard for a quarter.

"Richard! Heads, *Green Grow the Lilacs*, tails, *Dancing in the Streets*. Okay?"

"Okay."

I flipped the quarter with my right hand, hanging on for dear life to the telephone with the other. The quarter flip-flopped and settled tails up.

The try-outs of the two shows opened in Boston only a week apart. We were a great big smash hit, playing to standing-room only (possibly because I had recently finished my eleventh motion picture which was being shown at the movie theatre across the street), and we heard rumors that "*Lilacs*" still hadn't raised all its money. But Richard went to see their show one night and he came back full of excitement and almost speechless with the thrill it had been. He sensed what that show would mean to American theatre. It was only a few weeks later that we closed in Boston, never to open again. And they changed the title of their show to *Oklahoma!*

I couldn't do Oscar's face on his needlepoint pillow any more than I could anyone else's, but I always see that beautiful rugged face whenever I think of him or something he said. Like the night he saw *One Touch of Venus*. How his eyes twinkled when he said, "We saw the real Mary Martin in the last scene tonight. Sometime, I want to write a whole play about that Mary." What he meant by that would be a long story to explain, but years later, when he wrote the

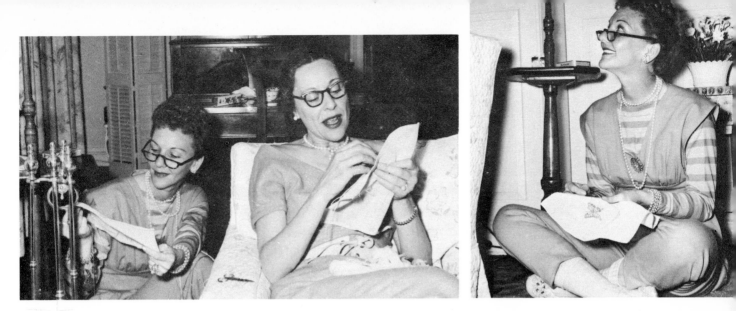

book for *South Pacific*, the part of Nellie Forbush made it clear to me what he meant. And the time he said, "Yes, I want to contribute to a production of *Peter Pan*. I want to hear all those children applauding when they help Peter to save Tinkerbell." I knew what he meant.

There was all that and more to think about as I was doing the needlepoint sketch of Oscar's tall figure in a big comfortable chair with his feet up, while his hands write out the lyrics of "Wonderful Guy" (color picture 12). The idea came from a wonderful photograph of him that is still in his study.

Who but Leland Hayward would pick up a phone and say, "Send a message, to all ships at sea. 'Are Richard Halliday and Mary Martin passengers on your ship?'" That is how Leland found us once, when, because of an irregularity of freighter schedules, we were taken off a boat in London and put on another that sailed within the hour. There had been no time to notify anyone where we were.

Some people have talent for singing, painting, acting, sculpture. There are many gifted artists, but in any field a great talent is rare. Leland has the greatest of all talents for using the telephone of anyone in our time. And I am serious. Whether a social, business, or professional call, if it is from Leland, you know at once something is going to happen.

Most businessmen spend hours over luncheon, cocktails, dinner, even late supper, meetings at their offices, writing memos and letters, *plus* a series of phone calls—all regarding one deal. Not Leland! One phone call, and before he has hung up, you have agreed to a deal. That is how many calls he and Richard exchanged about my appearing in *South Pacific*—one. It took one call for Leland to persuade Jerome Robbins that we would not do *Peter Pan* unless Jerry accepted his first assignment to direct as well as choreograph the production. Another time, Richard, Leland, and I had dinner together and among other things we told Leland I wanted more than anything to play the part of Maria von Trapp. We had bought the rights, but there were claims Richard had not cleared after nine months of negociating. The next afternoon, a phone call came from Leland. "How would you like a partner?" he asked Richard. "I'll fly to Berlin and clear up everything. Let's get started." Leland flew to Berlin. We started *The Sound of Music*.

We have talked to Leland by phone in New York, Connecticut, Beverly Hills, Hollywood, Paris, London, Rome, Cuba, Geneva, among other places, and something good, or or kind, or helpful—or exciting—has always come of it. Quite naturally, any "portrait" of Leland had to show him on the telephone. And for his pillow (color picture 14) I had him drawn sitting on a plain, high black stool because of the "all ships at sea" call which was about the 50th Ford Anniversary television show that Leland was producing, directed by Jerry Robbins. Ethel Merman and I were to appear on it together and we were to sing just one song. We rehearsed on high black stools and eventually performed on them. Then songs were added until there were dozens; we sat and rehearsed for days, weeks, and had a thrilling broadcast. Leland had brought about another hit.

Nancy, his wife (now Mrs. Kenneth Keith of London), is on the other end of the line. She was my first really professional needlepoint teacher and there is a piece of needlepoint in her lap. She is seldom without one. Her eyeglasses are pushed up high on her forehead. I'm not sure that she needlepoints while she talks on the telephone, but I'm sure she could if she wanted to. I can do one thing at a time; Nancy was never able to teach me to do three, four, five things at once as she does. I never take needlepoint out with me when I know I'll be with people, and I never bring a piece out when visitors call. I either get lost in doing the needlepoint or lost in the conversation.

But Nancy! At home, there she sits, hostess for a dinner of twelve or twenty-four. She talks to her guests on her right and on her left. She sips a dry martini, lights a cigarette, pulls her eyeglasses down from her forehead, and stitches away as she continues to listen and talk. Then she is at the door to greet new arrivals, she introduces them, sees that they have drinks, and returns to her needlepoint and conversation. All the while she is cool, colorful, fascinating, and in complete control of the occasion—and she has accomplished an inch or two or three of needlepoint before the front door closes behind the last guest to leave.

I can see that it is fun to do needlepoint the way Nancy does. Maybe you can work this way too, but don't be discouraged if you end up doing it my way. The important thing is to enjoy doing it, your way.

Josh! Joshua Logan. That fabulous dynamo of energy, vitality, personality, talent, a big man full of physical strength, yet sensitive, his ideas amazingly compound of words, music, movement, people, and pictures. It was a puzzlement to get even one small aspect of Josh down on a needlepoint canvas.

We were among a fortunate few to be there to see him use all his talents to their fullest one day when he started staging "There Is Nothing Like a Dame." No one who was there will ever forget the shock of excitement when from the back of the dimly lit rehearsal hall Josh's voice cracked out, "Play! Dames! Play! Play! Dames!" His voice sang the notes. He jumed out onto the floor. "Follow me! Follow me!" The piano played the music, Josh roared out the lyrics. He wove a pattern back and forth—upstage, downstage, stage right, stage left—"Follow me!" he shouted. "SeeBees! Right foot! Left foot!" He grabbed the young man nearest him, pulled him by his shirt, "Right! Left! Follow me!

There Is Nothing Like a Dame!" He grabbed another young man, "Here! March! March!" Singing, shouting instructions, Josh moved upstage, downstage without a pause, seemingly without taking a breath. The excitement filled the room and mounted to a deafening pitch as the piano pounded louder and louder and Josh's voice soared above everything. "Now! All together! Follow me!" He and the boys sang as their feet pounded "right foot, left foot" straight ahead until the pianist hit the last note—but Josh boomed out again, "Follow me! Again! Follow me!" and for the second time, and then for a third and fourth time, all the SeeBees followed Josh as he sang, shouted, led, directed, without pausing for one fraction of a second. And then he stopped and called out, "That's it!"

This is Josh. He is a huge canvas. How to capture any part of him on a tiny little needlepoint pillow? But then he did give me a key, another side of him, and all the pieces for a design fell into place. It was during our last rehearsal before the opening of *South Pacific* in London. Josh, the driving perfectionist, had made changes of places where I was to stand, to walk, to turn. After playing Nellie for two and a half years, I was finding it difficult to erase his previous directions and he could see this. I was growing very nervous and beginning to doubt that I would remember all the changes, when Josh came close to me on stage and said quietly,

> *"He who doubts from what he sees*
> *Will ne'er believe, do what you please.*
> *If the sun and moon should doubt,*
> *They'd immediately go out."*

Within the next few days, Richard began the design for Josh's pillow, the symbols of the poem in a needlepoint "stage" (color picture 15). There against the backdrop of blue sky is the red sun sinking below the rolling hills as, on the upper right, the crescent moon rises close to a star. The rows of poplar trees are the trees Josh especially loves to see along the country roads of France. The stream represents "real" effects in the theatre—we had often talked about how they can be used to communicate a special thrill to audiences, even streams and waterfalls and pools made with "real" water. And finally, around the "proceneum," we put in the turn-of-the-century red-velvet curtain with gold fringe to represent the grand tradition of theatre. It was just such a curtain that Josh bought during the production of *Kind Sir* so that he could have it installed in each theatre in which we appeared during the road tour before the New York opening.

On the reverse side of the pillow, I stitched a petit-point panel with the four lines by William Blake that Josh had quoted. I later heard him quote them again on several occasions, as he had done for me, to help a performer have confidence in herself.

Josh's dear wife, Nedda, has placed the pillow in their living room in New York, a room furnished with wonderful, colorful Victoriana and hung with part of their collection of very fine paintings. There is the pillow, and it is always a pleasant surprise to me to see that it holds its own even in that extraordinary and brilliantly successful room.

....

The first three "*South Pacific*" pillows were all done in about the same way. We found photographs from which drawings could be made, and the designs were traced for me on canvas from the drawings by a professional—only in dark-grey lines, no color or shading. The neutral color schemes I worked out myself and they were really inspired by the neutral black-and-white of the photographs, but in warmer tones.

Dick Rodgers's pillow was done on fourteen-stitch-to-the-inch double canvas, which split into tiny twenty-eight stitches to the inch for the petit point that sketches Dick and his hands and the music he is writing. The background is fourteen-stitch needlepoint. Oscar's and Leland and

Nancy's pillows were done on twelve-stitch-to-the-inch double canvas, split for petit point for the figures with the larger needlepoint again used for the backgrounds. The petit point really does look finer and clearer set in a background of coarser needlepoint.

The pillow for Josh Logan was something else again. Richard did the initial sketch which we had transferred to canvas for us, in color. I did not follow the colors very literally, for all sorts of ideas came up. In the details such as the sun and moon, the poplars, the running stream, and the gold fringe of the curtain, I worked in petit point in both silk and wool. In the stream, especially, the shimmer of silk gives an amusing effect of "real" water. This is a twelve-stitch-to-the-inch double canvas. Most of the curtain, sky, and field are in twelve-stitch needlepoint, and in the field I tried something new. Many of the gradations of color were achieved not simply by changing wool colors, but by mixing two strands of one color with one strand of another (in other words, assembling a three-strand thread of normal weight from separated strands of different colors). Close to, this can be seen, but from a very short distance away the colors meld into gradations you can get no other way. You can achieve unusual irridescent effects by mixing colors this way and some of the sparkle of that pillow is due to this. You can also get muddy colors. I know of no rule except trial and error to control this. Appropriately enough, this needlepoint "stage set" for Josh is as close to "painted" as anything I have ever stitched.

The
Grecian rugs

If I've given the impression that doing needlepoint is *always* the greatest fun, the most joyous pastime, that everyone should love doing it more than anything else in the world— let me say quickly that's not true—not always. Of course it can be tedious. Twice, for very long periods, I had to manufacture more patience within myself than I thought I was capable of, I had to discipline myself and force myself, in the name of love, to finish what I had begun.

The first time was when I thought of the two Grecian rugs of black and beige and terra cotta for Richard—for his bath-dressing room. He would like the design and the colors, which were also ideal for the room. I took measurements, drew up the classic design, had the beige wool dyed exactly the unobtainable shade I wanted, and began the stitches with all the excitement that accompanies each new project. I stitched one of the long lines of beige, and I stitched a black oblong, and my mind began to wander. I used some of the terra cotta for a change, but the pattern called for only a few lines of it—so I returned to the black, then beige, and I felt very dull. I found myself thinking of the thousands upon thousands of needlepoint pieces that are sold at department stores and needlework shops across the country—the ones that have the design already stitched, leaving only the background for the purchaser to fill in. This I have never understood; it is the design that is challenging and the most fun of all. Even the most conventional design of a tulip, for instance, for which you are usually given two shades of yel-

low for the flower and two shades of green for the leaves—
Oh! the fun of discovering for yourself that three shades of
yellow and three of green are far more effective. There are
times when four shades of each are still better, and I've
experimented with five. One day, I hope to do a huge coral
rose in full bloom that will need six different coral shades
plus two shades of white.

But at this particular moment I was stuck with solid beige,
solid black, a tiny amount of terra cotta. I tried thinking of
myself as a calm, contented, loving wife who adored taking
every stitch. I was quite unsuccessful in the role.

Unconsciously (at least, I prefer to think it was an un-
conscious campaign), I seemed to be in a period when I
thought everyone would thank me for the rest of their lives
if I taught them how to do needlepoint. What better way
than to have them learn on these very two rugs? There was
one late Saturday night, when a famous dress designer drove
to the country with us after the show to spend the week
end. During supper, I talked about needlepoint and soon I
had one of the rugs out to demonstrate, and the next moment
I suggested that she try it. The next morning, when we came
down to breakfast, there she was sitting in the same chair
with the rug limply hanging across her lap. She was limp,
too, and she was pale grey with red rims around her glazed
eyes. She had worked, mesmerized, through the night, stitching too tightly, struggling to take the stitches out, only to
make the next stitches too loose, etc., etc., into the early
morning hours. Now she rose weakly from the chair and
in an almost inaudible whisper said, "You've made a terrible,
terrible mistake, Mary," and disappeared into her room for
the rest of the day.

Another time, Shirley Booth seemed so eager to stitch in
one of the black sections—or perhaps I was the one who
was eager for her to put one in. No matter, when she had
finally finished it, she announced, "That is the first and last
time I'll ever try that kind of thing—for posterity, I put in
my initials." You will see, if you look carefully, the initials

S.B. in the corner of one black oblong. But then, not long after, we phoned to speak to Shirley Booth about something or other, and we heard, "No, Miss Booth isn't in." "No, I don't know when she'll be back. She went to that place to see about getting more of that needlepoint thing she's doing"! In the next rug, you'll notice two of the oblongs were filled in with designs. These represent lessons done

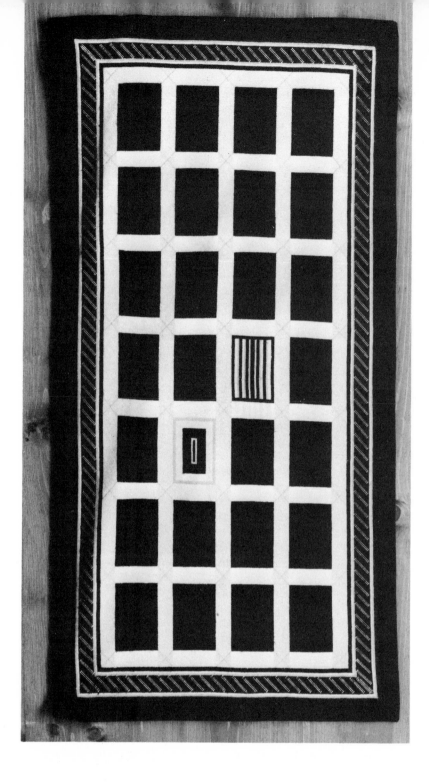

by different dear friends who had different ideas, some of whom are now avid needlepointers.

Those rugs! If we hadn't taken a freighter trip on which we spent as many as ten days at a time without landing, I wonder if they would ever have been finished. The sun and sea and air worked miracles to help make the beige lines, the black oblongs less monotonous to get through.

58

By the time the rugs were finished, I had learned two things. First, the original idea was a good one. Richard obviously has enjoyed them in the room he uses constantly. I frequently hear him say, "These were a gift from my wife Mary," in the tone that makes every wife warm and happy. On the other hand, I learned that for me plain needlepointing is a monotonous, ungratifying bore. And the more needlepoint I do, I find I like more and more design which covers almost the entire surface. It is altogether rewarding to think of a design, draw a sketch, and see what happens as the shades of wool or silk or cotton fill in all the little sections of color. The best part of doing any background is watching the stitches gradually surround the design.

....

Even though these rugs were so laborious to do, and big (two and a half feet by five feet), if you like the design, it certainly would be easy to copy. It would not take long to do a small, stylish modern pillow of let us say twelve oblongs with a border (the darker of the two borders), copied directly from the photograph. Anyone who has mastered the basketweave stitch (page 138) and understands how stitches line up with each other diagonally, as well as up and down, on a canvas could recreate the design in a trice. Keep it small. Make the oblongs two by three inches at the most, with about one and a half inches or less of beige between them. Make the fine diagonal lines (grey in the photograph) terra cotta. Everything will fit together perfectly. Any rank beginner, perhaps with a more experienced needlepointing friend to advise and help sketch the design on canvas, could do it. If you've done much needlepoint, even the sketch might not be necessary; you could work on blank canvas and merely do a little counting of stitches to make sure everything lines up. If you want to do a border of the bolder beige-and-black motif, it should be drawn on the canvas as those stripes are not exactly on the forty-five-degree diagonal of the canvas mesh.

16–Heller's christening dress, on the right, which my mother made, and the party dress, which Mainbocher made for Heller when she was just three, both helped to inspire the wedding jacket.

17–This is the jacket I made for our daughter Heller's wedding. It is a copy of an evening jacket of mine, designed by Mainbocher, recut in needlepoint canvas and then stitched all over in plain white, with only the petit-point button and flowers tied with "something-blue" ribbons on the sleeves for decoration.

The wedding jacket, "All on my fingers"

It was my mother who made the lovely, simple white batiste dress for Heller's christening which now hangs framed in our bedroom for me to see every day.

Because I come from Texas, and Richard does not, when I showed him the dress, we had one of the few conversations we have ever had in which we did not seem to understand each other. "Look! Richard," I exclaimed, "She did all of it on her fingers!" Richard got that patient look one sometimes sees on a husband's face.

"What you mean is, your mother made this by hand?"

"By hand? That sounds ridiculous."

"Didn't you wear handmade clothes that your mother sewed when you were a little girl?"

"Heavens, no! I'm explaining, Richard, that she did it all on her fingers. Every Texas mother sews on her fingers."

"But, Mary, what about the expression 'handsewn' . . ." He got no further.

"Never mind. I never was able to learn to do anything on my fingers anyway, so we just won't have to talk about it again."

But we did, because I never got over wanting to do *something* all on my fingers, which is why Richard eventually thought of needlepoint and The Family Rug. So Heller's

18–On the preceding pages, a needlework fantasy in honor of two of my most treasured possessions, the lace bedspread my mother made for me and the silk petit-point pillow I made for Richard's mother. Their stories begin on page 65.

19–Detail of the wedding jacket.

christening dress has a great deal to do with my interest in needlepoint, and the other framed dress has a special connection, too. It was made by Mainbocher, as a surprise to Heller's parents, for her third-birthday party—exquisitely dainty and extravagant, a whisp of dotted Swiss organdy embroidered with small flowers with petals of hand-appliquéd gold and white crystals. Years later, when Heller was about fourteen, Mainbocher made something marvellous for me, a short gray evening jacket so beautifully cut and becoming that it made me feel young and gay and ready for a party just to put it on. Naturally, Heller wanted to see how it looked on her and it had a perfection all its own for her, too. Then she spoke again of the day, someday, when she would walk down the aisle of a church to marry the man she loved. She frequently referred to this distant time in those days, and, standing there beside her in front of the mirror, I let my imagination follow hers for a moment. I saw our little daughter grown up, coming down the aisle in her white wedding dress and—a white jacket, in a white jacket exactly like this one, made by me, all in needlepoint. Yes! And where Mainbocher had put delicate embroidery of silver and "diamonds" on each sleeve, I would do sprays of blue and pink and green petit-point flowers and leaves with blue ribbons. At last, I had thought of something I could make for *my* daughter that might compare with some of the tens upon tens of dresses and robes and petticoats my mother had made for me. Mainbocher was as enthusiastic as I was. In fact, years later, he began the design for a wedding dress to be worn with the jacket.

Yes, it took years. Young as Heller was, I had started none too soon. Over what seemed to be the acres of the pieces of the jacket pattern, I was stitching away again with love along one endless row of white stitches after the next. It took

61

John Engstead photo-
graphed me in 1956 with all
the needlepoint he could
squeeze into the picture.
The Rug had long since
been finished and I had
recently begun the petit
point for the sleeves of
Heller's wedding jacket.

years in New York, while the white wool became various
shades of grey from the soot that fell from the city sky as I
stitched away on our terrace garden. It took months in Brazil,
where it became reddish brown while I stitched away on it
at Nossa Fazenda. We were there during the dry season, and
this was before any of the roads had been paved, when even
if there should be an hour's downpour, within the next hour
great clouds of red dust swirled into the sky whenever a
horse, a jeep, or a herd of cattle went down the road. Although the main road was two miles from the house, even so,
imperceptible particles accumulated to color the white wool.

As I took one white stitch and another and another and
another, I wondered if I would ever take the last one in time
for our young lady—not our little girl, for she was sixteen
by now—for her to wear the jacket at her wedding two,
four, six, how many years from now? I loved making the
petit-point sprays on the sleeves and the button at the collar.
But as the months and years passed, and though I worked on
many other pieces, too, I was always aware that I must return
to the endless white stitches. Over a period of four years,
while I appeared in New York and also traveled and toured
(and learned to needlepoint and watch TV at the same time;
that helped), I stitched away, while our daughter fell in and
out of love. When the day of real love finally came, and
the date was set, the last stitch *had* been taken, the Scala-
mandré silk lining had been selected, all the pieces had been
assembled, and the jacket was ready. And what did they do?
They eloped!

Mainbocher may have thought the needlepoint jacket was
a good idea, but the designer at Mazaltov's needlepoint shop
who had to help me with it said it simply couldn't be done.
But she couldn't bear not to meet the challenge—she had
conquered all our other strange needlepointing requests—

62

and almost overnight the problem was solved after all. The grey jacket was completely taken apart, the pieces pressed, and the pattern of each one traced on canvas—a rather fine fourteen-stitch-to-the-inch white single canvas to be worked with a two-strand wool thread rather than the usual three strands. This meant a lot of white stitches to the inch, but a coarser canvas and heavier wool would have made too stiff and heavy a fabric. As it is, the flairing shape of the jacket still stands out just as it was designed to do even though it has been worn and worn (and recently taken apart to be washed and reassembled).

When they are finished, the pieces of anything as complicated as this should be blocked by a professional, for they become distorted as they are worked and must be gotten back exactly to the shapes of the original pattern. And as I, unlike Heller, still could not sew particularly well, these needlepoint pieces were assembled as well as blocked at Mazaltov's. My son Larry's wife, Maj, sews beautifully, too, and she put in the silk lining for me, using the lining of the original grey jacket as a guide.

In other words, for the needlepointer, a jacket such as this really is very simple and logical. You just start with a garment that fits beautifully in the first place, trace the pattern exactly, and then stitch away, with love and perseverance. I do suggest that something with more design on it would be more fun, but of course this jacket had to be white. Then, more skilled hands than mine must put it all together. Not every needlepoint shop will have someone available who can tailor a jacket, so you might have to have the pieces blocked first, and then go to a good tailor for the final assembly.

The violet pillow and the lace spread

London, 1952. One of those justifiably famous spring days. A warm, golden sun, and wherever we looked there were flowers—in window boxes of houses and stores, masses of blooms in every park between great expanses of rich green lawns, and there were wooden carts in the streets loaded with both vegetables and flowers. From one of them, a stranger impetuously handed me the most luxurious, luscious, the biggest, the most violet-scented bunch of violets I have ever seen. Perhaps because the first time I met Richard's mother, she was wearing a spring hat made of violets, I decided to capture this bouquet for her in needlepoint. At the Royal School of Needlework at Prince's Gate, with the help of Miss Ward and other members of the staff, we made sketches for a petit-point canvas and chose samples of green and violet and mauve silk—the first silk thread I had ever used.

Thirteen years later, I had finished the pillow in color picture 18. Despite all that time, this proved to be one of the three or four most gratifying pieces of work I have done. Although my mood had to be exactly right—and the proper light was equally necessary!—it was a pleasure to use the soft silk thread. I carried the canvas with me constantly during our travels and just occasionally, when I was completely relaxed, I enjoyed stitching with the fine silk for an hour but seldom longer. Richard's mother was patient, very

In the New York
apartment, the Aubusson
tapestry, the lace spread,
and the silk violet pillow.

patient indeed. She was the only member of the family who wasn't surprised when the violets received first prize at their first showing. "You didn't need anyone to tell you that would happen, did you? No surprise to me!"

From the first day I met her, I wanted to give her first prize for being a great mother-in-law. In fact, both Richard and I were fortunate. We each had a great mother-in-law. Even if you do not believe in astrology (and even those who don't seem to wonder—"I don't believe in it, but sometimes I think there *must* be *something* about it!"), it is interesting to know that they were born in the same month of the same year, within the same week. An astrologer would assume they had similar characteristics. They did. They were wonderfully active, interested, and interesting women. They were doers, they were creative, they loved making a home for their families, and, bless them both, they were independent. And they were givers, too. There were many holidays and special days which one or the other of them made into memorable occasions—but also they both had a way of slipping into an ordinary, average day a moment to remember.

On one such day, when Richard and I came home in the evening and walked into our bedroom, we literally did gasp for breath at the sight of the beautiful écru silk and lace spread that had appeared on the bed. It was so lovely, so handsome, but in addition it had something all its own. It had been made with love. Nanny, my mother, had sewed it—all on her fingers. You can see a swirl of one small section of the lace and of the pleated-silk flounce in the picture of Mammy's, Richard's mother's, silk violet pillow. This example of Nanny's stitching-to-perfection is a personal creation that we admire and use every ordinary, average day that we are home. And, like Heller's christening dress that my mother made, it prods me gently to stitch something, too, in my own way. I often think of the bedspread when I am doing a particularly difficult section of needlepoint. I thought of it often as I slowly, slowly finished Mammy's violet pillow.

Working silk petit point is a matter of two things—the very best materials, and patience. Under the heading of materials, add also that for such a special project you might as well invest in a design, whatever its source, that is drawn on the canvas for you with care by a good professional. The best silk seems to be imported, and you need the best, for silk, even of the finest quality, tends to fray as you work with it. It is quite scarce in this country and I have heard experienced needlepointers advise that you buy good silk whenever you come across it, whether you have a particular project in mind for it or not, as you may not find it when you start to look for it.

For the violet pillow, I used a smooth linen single canvas with a twenty-four-stitch-to-the-inch mesh (page 130). The silk thread covered it perfectly, and you should test how your silk covers the canvas you choose before you go ahead with the design. Of course, you must use a fine needle, but use a thin embroidery needle with a slightly blunt point, as too sharp a point splits the delicate threads of neighboring stitches as you fit new stitches in next to them. Go to any lengths to have perfect light to work by, and then just relax, enjoy the lovely texture of the silk stitches as they fill in the canvas one tiny area at a time, and give up all thought of hurrying. It can't be done.

The "leaf" border on the violet pillow is a motif Richard first designed for this pillow. As you can see on pages 32 and 130, I used it again on a rug canvas.

In our sky-high, soft-sky-blue bedroom in New York, we still use Nanny's spread of many laces, and now Mammy's violet pillow is there, too, resting against the bolster. So delicate is the texture of the lace against the écru silk backing that you can barely see in the photograph on page 67 how it extends in a broad panel the full length of the bed. All that lace once belonged to my mother, my sister, or me. It is made of pieces that were originally used on dresses, underwear, a hat or two, blouses, all of which were made by Nanny. Unknown to any of us, for years she had rescued all those bits and pieces and yards of lace and kept them.

Some people like to do crossword puzzles, or play solitaire or bridge. "I'd rather be doing things," Nanny would say. We learned later that she had first made a large pattern on brown paper. On quiet afternoons or evenings, she spread it on the living-room floor and patiently fitted and pinned the pieces together on it. This was her lacey, memory-laden jigsaw puzzle. The pieces didn't always fit the pattern. I really can see Nanny—gently placing a piece of lace in position, standing up, looking down, walking around full circle, stopping to see the effect from every angle and, not pleased, bending down to move the piece to another spot a second, third, fourth time, until each piece of lace belonged with the next. Satisfied at long last, she began taking all the tiny stitches— all on her fingers—that hold the many fragments together as if they were one.

Just so that I do not give the impression that Nanny was a darling, quiet, little old Texas lady who was content with her sewing and knitting and flowers, I would like to add that I have seen those small hands grasp the wheel of an automobile with all the strength of a truck driver. As I held my breath, away we would go, around corners, across the streets of Weatherford, Fort Worth, Hollywood, Beverly Hills, speeding along highways, passing cars and trucks, and every time, when we got to our destination, Nanny would look at her watch and say with satisfaction, "Yes! Made it on time!" She was a woman of many talents.

The bedroom in our New York apartment has in it today some of the purchases Richard and I made for our first home, among them the tapestry on the wall behind the bed. This was our problem child, an Aubusson tapestry originally made for the Duke and Duchess of Marlboro; see the "M" below the crown at the top. Richard bought it as a surprise, claiming it was made for Mary or for the Martins of Weatherford, Texas. I became especially interested in it later when I started to do needlepoint and saw in the weaving of the tapestry how wool colors work into a design. Eventually, I copied the "M" for the seat cushion of the low French chair on page 94.

But meanwhile, the Aubusson had had its drawbacks. Originally, we had the problem of height; we had no room high enough in which to hang this richly handsome piece. We got to know its measurements by heart as we moved from one place to the next in which it would not fit. One of the many reasons we were enthusiastic about the New York penthouse was that when we measured this wall we knew the tapestry would fit, at last.

But our hearts sank when we saw it hung in place. We had not realized how heavy the regal but blackish-red borders would look until we saw it in our skylike room. In desperation, I took it from one specialist to another, asking to have the dreary red border cut away. Every time, and rightly, of course, each expert I approached refused. They were shocked at the very idea, and it was not too long before I felt shocked at myself for thinking of it.

It was a needlepoint expert, a quiet, dear, elderly woman, trained abroad, who thought of the solution. She asked permission to experiment and sewed a perfectly cut border of dull blue satin over every bit of the gloomy dark red, fitting it meticulously around the swags and bits of design at the edges of the original border. There it is, still quite grand but light and airy, with the equally light-hearted pair of angels brought to us by Nancy and Leland Hayward from Italy, and framing a Christmas gift from Dorothy Hammerstein, "The Lady After Her Bath" by Phillips.

The
chair seat
that grew

During the first year of *The Sound of Music*, on one of my perennial trips to Mazaltov's to match yarn, I saw a square canvas painted with a bunch of asparagus tied with ribbons of the loveliest shade of red. I immediately fell in love with the design and the colors, dropped what I had been doing, and started working on the new canvas.

A few evenings later, as I stitched on the needlepoint asparagus and chatted with Richard about the real asparagus he had planted at the farm in Brazil, it occurred to me that a series of vegetables would be ideal for the dining-room chairs at Nossa Fazenda. Within days we had five more canvases with designs of artichokes, onions, celery, carrots, and a cabbage. We agreed on a bright yellow background for them and hoped there would be time to finish all six before we went back to Brazil.

Not more than three weeks later, Richard bought a collection of perfectly lovely old French color prints of luscious fruits—grapes, pears, cherries, plums, peaches, and many more—for the dining room in New York. They are perfect for the French and Italian furniture we have there, but when they were first hung something seemed to have gone wrong. The French Empire chest looked less handsome, our Italian piecrust table less lovely—everything in the room had somehow lost character. We soon saw that the carpet was responsible. It had been used in five different rooms over a period of years and the fresh colors in those old prints plainly showed up how dull it had become.

As I am never without a piece of needlepoint on Sunday, every performer's treasured day off, I had the artichoke square with me at the supper table one Sunday evening a few weeks later. It fell on the tired greyish-green carpet, and at that very moment, I remember, irrelevantly, Richard was finishing our favorite dessert of vanilla ice cream with hot fudge sauce and toasted almonds. "Richard," I asked, pointing to the artichoke, "Can a chair seat grow into a rug?" One of the great satisfactions of a lasting marriage is the mutual understanding of this sort of shorthand language. Richard took a brief glance at the needlepoint on the floor and got up to get a pad and pencil.

We made many sketches for the rug that night and finally Richard drew up the "simple, practical solution." By this he meant a rug we would never be afraid to walk on, on which we would not hesitate to draw our chairs to and from the table. And so evolved the border of needlepoint squares inlaid in plain carpeting, with an extra square inside each of the four corners and an ample island of carpeting in the center. There would be plenty of room for guests to twist and turn and push back their chairs without chair legs or a lady's narrowest high heel getting caught between stitches.

Now, according to the design before us, we had progressed

from a single square of asparagus, to six chair seats that would never be, to a series of twenty-six squares for a whole new rug. The most fun to do were the pineapple, the watermelon (since I am a native of Weatherford, Texas, where they grow the biggest watermelons in the world, it was a must), the artichokes, avocados (we grow the most delicious ones in Brazil, eight inches long, and they are so good it is a crime to put any kind of dressing on them, even a drop of lemon), the strawberries, casaba melon, cauliflower, celery and, of course, the asparagus. The two that proved to be most diffi-cult were the bananas and the grapes. Didi, Richard's sister, valiantly tried to finish the bananas and put in and took out innumerable stitches. The grapes were a problem that was never properly solved; I tried to be too subtle in the shading and didn't outline each grape with a yarn dark enough to give them shape.

At last, at long last, all the squares were done. We had decided the wool rug in which they were to be set had to be the same shade of yellow as the background of the needle-point. From a collection of rug samples we chose the perfect match and sent for a large piece to experiment with. I care-fully placed the asparagus in the center. There was a heavy silence. I added the pineapple and the watermelon. We didn't

73

say a word. We put a dozen more squares around the yellow sample. We looked at the design and at last at each other. We were keenly disappointed. Perhaps it would be better to look at it in the daylight.

We finally gave up on the yellow carpeting. It did nothing for our design nor for the room itself. Perhaps the brilliant green that appeared most frequently in the needlepoint would be right. We chose a green rug sample, and this time we experimented by cutting a square out of it and sewing the asparagus into place. Yes! Yes? Something was still missing. We stood looking—looking at the walls and the prints and back down at the asparagus square. Then the brass-bamboo step-railing that leads to the terrace caught my eye. It brought to mind the avenue of bamboo trees through which we drive on the way to the house in Brazil, which in turn reminded me of the little antique bamboo-turned high chair the Leland Hayward's had given us at Christmas . . .

The next morning I entered Mazaltov's with the bamboo chair and the twenty-six finished pieces of needlepoint. There was, I pointed out, enough of the canvas mesh left around the squares so that each one could be framed in a bamboo design in needlepoint exactly the width of the slender bamboo of the chair. It was almost like starting at the beginning again. Twenty-six bamboo frames all exactly alike! But it was worth it. The moment the last stitch had been taken on the first square, we put it on the green carpet sample and we knew that we finally had the solution to the rug that we would enjoy for years to come.

Or so we thought until Mr. Rosenfield of the Stark Rug Company phoned several months later. He had often gone out of his way to help us solve our rug problems, and of course, when the needlepoint squares were done, he was in charge of having them inserted properly in the green carpet. There didn't seem to be the usual spark in his voice this time. He kept talking in circles, not really saying anything, but still talking. He was indignant. I heard, ". . . which is far, far too much to pay. It's ridiculous! It's out of the question!

On a freighter trip to Brazil —sun, sea, air, and needle-point—I can't imagine a better way to travel. This was taken in 1963 before we returned to New York for the rehearsals of Jennie; *the needlepoint is one of the last squares of the dining room rug.*

How could we possibly enjoy a rug at that price?!" (Mr. Rosenfield becomes so genuinely involved in our decorating decisions that he always says "we" as if he, too, would have to live with the results.) His voice rose. "What do they think, it's to be hung in a museum?!" At that point, I suggested he talk to Richard. It was some time before they hung up and Richard announced pessimistically, "Well, it's the cost of the labor . . . he thinks he has a solution. We'll see. He'll be here tomorrow."

Mr. Rosenfield proposed a remarkable solution he had worked out, to send the needlepoint squares and the carpet all the way across the country and across the Pacific to Hong Kong to be made up. I was horrified. All those months and months of work; whose hands would it fall into! (This was five years before I first went to Hong Kong, during our tour of *Hello, Dolly!* and my idea of Hong Kong was more like something in "Terry and the Pirates" than the fascinating city I later discovered.) What about workmanship? Both Mr. Rosenfield and Richard assured me that Hong Kong had many more gifted artisans than Oriental villains and that the needlepoint would be insured (though I still can't see, if anything had gone wrong, what insurance could have done to replace all those stitches). "It's the only way WE can afford the rug," Mr. Rosenfield kept repeating. "Half the

75

20—*Needlepoint is a very tough material but nevertheless not really practical for a dining-room rug. Our solution for our dining room in New York was a border of needlepoint squares inlaid around the edge of a brilliant green carpet. The dining table and chairs stand in the island of plain carpeting in the middle.*

21, 22, & 23—*On the following pages: left, the watermelon square and the lemon square; opposite, the picture shows how we elaborated on the border design by putting an extra needlepoint square in each corner of the rug. The first square had originally been intended for a set of six chair seats, but it grew into a series of twenty-six fruits and vegetables for the rug instead.*

price of doing it here, the price you were counting on, even with the shipping!" They finally convinced me this was the only reasonable thing to do, and I let Mr. Rosenfield send the twenty-six needlepoint squares away.

For the next year, there was no time to think about them again. There were rehearsals for a new show, *Jennie*, a long and particularly difficult tryout period on the road, the New York opening and, after a brief run, we flew to Brazil again for a rest. The highlight of our return to New York was to see the dining room at the apartment complete. The rug had arrived safely, by freighter, and it was a great success.

Opening night for the rug was the very next day when my son Larry, with his wife Maj and our grandchildren, Heidi and Preston, joined us for dinner. Maj was nervous for fear Preston, age three, would drop hamburger or green peas on the new rug. Both Richard and I assured her we wanted this rug to be enjoyed. No one was to worry. The subject was dropped and practically no one stopped talking as there was so much to tell and to ask about the family, Larry's work, our farm. We were so busy making up for lost time that no one noticed Preston had left the table until he returned from the kitchen, walking very slowly, carrying in both hands a dish of ice cream and cake. Meeri, the maid, followed behind, proudly supervising his progress.

"Careful, Preston," Maj said.

Preston looked up with his angelic smile. We started to talk again and then we heard a thump. It was obvious what had happened. I quickly looked at Richard. He had just as quickly averted his eyes and continued calmly to talk to Larry. Hurriedly, I picked up my conversation. "Maj!

76

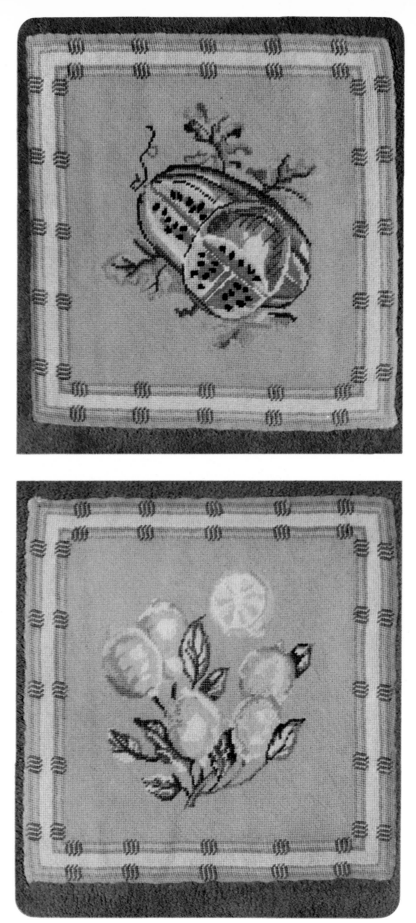

21

22

23

24

24—We have a remarkable flock of parakeets that often comes to rest on the tree tops at the farm in Brazil. There are thousands of them and they so impressed us that I felt I had to do some of my best petit point in their honor (page 79).

You've got to see the most wonderful new cotton material they are making in Brazil. I've brought some back for you . . ."

But Maj couldn't stand the suspense another moment. She looked around to see Preston watching Meeri who had quickly brought a bowl of water, a sponge, a clean cloth. The ice cream and cake were back in the dish. Meeri was lightly patting the needlepoint beets with the cloth.

"Let's have coffee in the living room." I was determined to get us out before anyone looked more carefully.

Richard got up. "I haven't shown you the pictures I took this time . . ." He was standing with his back to the beets.

"You must see them, Larry," I urged. "Come on, Maj, I'll show you the material."

Suddenly a new voice spoke. "Look! See!" We all stopped and turned toward Meeri. She was smiling, pointing to the beets. "See, they are all clean again, ready to cook now." All four of us took a deep breath, slowly walked across the room, slowly looked down, leaned down, got on our knees.

"I don't believe it, Meeri!" Maj said.

"It was easy," said Meeri.

"Of course it was," I added. "This is a practical rug. You don't think we'd have anything but a practical rug in the dining room, do you? With grandchildren running around?"

It had been a long and involved affair, that "simple, practical solution" to turning one little chair seat into a large dining-room rug. So we are very, very grateful to Preston for proving on its first night that we are really practical grandparents after all.

. . . .

For those who might like to use Richard's idea of needlepoint inlaid in carpeting, I certainly would like to point out that we think it could be done on a much smaller scale and without resorting to having the rug mounted on the other side of the world. You probably are aware that sets of needlepoint squares, six, nine, even twelve of them, each square with a different design on one general theme, are sold in needlework shops to be sewed together when they are done into all-over needlepoint rugs. You can also have these squares designed according to your own ideas, which is even more fun. There is no reason why just six squares could not be turned into a good-size area rug or a marvellous narrow runner six squares long. There would be the obvious advantage that you would not have to stitch every square inch of the rug, which might be as big as five by seven feet. More interesting, though, is the rich effect of the closely stitched needlepoint framed in the deep pile of the carpeting. The textures are lovely, and you might work out a needlepoint border for the squares that would set them off in such a way that you *could* have the rug and the background of the needlepoint inside the border of the same color—as we tried to do with our first yellow rug sample before we had to switch to green.

To give you some idea of dimensions, most such squares measure about eighteen inches (though what is to prevent you from having any size or shape you want?). The canvas is "rug" canvas, ten stitches to the inch (mine was white single canvas, fast and easy to work on). As my experience proved, it is a good idea to have plenty of extra canvas all around the designs in case you become involved in an additional border design. The pieces of needlepoint need to be spaced far enough apart in the final rug so that the bands of carpeting between them are effective. When the needlepoint is mounted in the rug, the workmen remove areas of the pile just the size of the squares, which are then sewn into place so that they really are "inlaid" in it.

The
parakeet pillow

A pillow that had to be is the one of the parakeets in color picture 24. The birds sit on limbs that represent the bamboos which line the road to our house in Brazil, against a blue that cannot properly reproduce the clear, shining blue skies of our state of Goias. The birds are only eight, but they represent the thousands of parakeets that zoom across the sunrise at the farm for approximately six weeks of every year—screaming, shrieking at the tops of their tiny lungs.

The parakeets have chosen Nossa Fazenda for their resting, breathing spot. On some unseen signal, they land on the tops of the huge old, deep-green mango trees between the house and the pond, and there is a sudden stillness that makes one aware of the whole sky and all the earth below. Gradually, there come chirping sounds, then the same loud screech, and they streak away, thousands of tiny jewel-colored arrows. They disappear into the clear sky within seconds. At sunset, exactly on time, we hear them returning, we see their small forms land again on the mango trees. We feel the sudden stillness once more, and then we know from the increasing chirping that they have caught their breaths and will soon zoom up, away, screaming out their shrill goodnight.

It was several years before we learned from a rice farmer miles west of us that while we were enjoying the parakeets' greeting twice a day, he was roundly cursing them. "The darling, pretty little things, indeed!" They were coming to his land all day to eat every bit of rice they possibly could before the harvest. Every evening they flew off to their home, wherever it was, by way of our mango trees, but they returned to his precious rice each morning. It was too late by the time the farmer told us what a problem they can be. We loved them and they had long since been immortalized in petit point; I finished them during a long freighter trip headed south of the equator.

This pillow, like so many pillows, belongs in a particular chair, the lounge chair in the plant room off our bedroom. The pillow supports the back firmly, a good book is always kept here, and this is the ideal reading corner at the farm. The chair itself was made for us by Altamira, the carpenter, who over the years has also made cattle guards, chicken runs, cow sheds—constructed the roofs over all the animals' heads as well as over our own—and made most of the cabinets, closets, tables, and chairs. There would not even be a place to put a needlepoint pillow at the farm without Altamira!

....

The background around the petit-point birds is in larger needlepoint; this was a standard fourteen-stitch-to-the-inch double canvas, which splits into twenty-eight tiny stitches to the inch for petit point. The design is a good example of why one need not do things the hard way. It could have been done, to make it into a display of patience and perseverance, on a fine twenty-four-mesh or more single canvas, in other words the equivalent of petit point over every square inch, background and all.

It is not an excuse for laziness but a fact that the contrasting larger background stitch makes the birds look even more delicate than they would with the blue sky done in the same tiny stitch—which is also rather difficult to work smoothly in wool over large plain areas. In general, I think all-over petit point is best for a design that fills almost all the space, with very little background. But neither am I much tempted by such laborious projects. Of course, there has been at least one notable exception, the violet pillow (color picture 18). But that was special, my great experiment in working with silk, which, if you can muster the patience, produces the smoothest, loveliest petit point that can be made.

The angel pillows

Pillows! The word is almost synonymous with needlepoint. Every now and then I do get just a little down on pillows— or, at least, it gives me an added feeling of accomplishment when a good reason comes along to do something entirely different: the panels for Vossa Casa, Heller's jacket, the very sentimental rocker, rugs. . . . But those are long projects and ideas keep coming for needlepoint. Most of them would never even be tried if it weren't for lovely, practical, quick pillows to experiment on. And besides, many of the best ideas for needlepoint designs are nevertheless more appropriate for modest pillows than for elaborate projects. And so I have done pillows and pillows and pillows — most needlepointers do — I still never seem to run out of places to put them or people to give them to, and once I even went so far as to do four of them all alike.

Perhaps you have seen Degas's sculptures of ballet dancers, or photographs of them—the young dancers with ballet skirts made of actual material. Those figures cast a spell never to be forgotten, and we were reminded of them when Janet Gaynor brought still another of her gifts to us for the farm in Brazil. She came into the house holding a box about the size of a shoe box, with the top off. On the crisp white tissue paper inside was an angel in French-blue robes that seemed poised to fly out and away up into the sky. The modeling of this seventeenth-century angel's face and golden wings was in almost perfect condition, only the coloring had softened with the years. The folds of the robe, made of fine cotton, fell in lovely long lines that gave the figure the motion of flying. There were a few tiny holes in the cloth which was almost as crisp as the tissue paper, and we were immediately aware that the robes could be touched only tenderly and very occasionally.

Janet had found our angel in Bahia, the colorful old city on the northwest coast of Brazil where the Portuguese originally settled, and where today there are 365 elaborate churches to attend—one for each day in the year. We hung the angel against the white wall at one end of the living room where she still seems always to be in flight, towards the tall glass doors that open onto the terrace. Three or four times each year we have a blowing contest. No one is allowed to touch the angel, but we watch with concern to see who can blow off the greatest amount of dust from her flowing robes. And each year we dread to look closer for fear we will discover another tiny hole or small crack in the material. We wished we could somehow preserve the figure more permanently or give it the good company of companion angels. We were talking about this one day and also about what we should do for the empty green living-room couch. Of course! Angel pillows, of many colors. We lifted our angel gently from the wall, placed it on a cloth on the floor, and took photographs looking straight down at her, or him (there is still a difference of opinion in the family as to whether angels are all "her" or "him"). Later, from an enlarged photograph, we drew the figure on four needlepoint canvases—double canvas, to split for petit-point angels against backgrounds of fourteen-stitches-to-the-inch needlepoint. We chose the colors that you see in color pictures 25 and 26 from the window curtains, pink, blue, and lavender and shades of green.

Each angel was a challenge; each sash and robe, I was determined, would be more flowing, more graceful than the

82

25—The design for these four angels came from a seventeenth-century figure that Janet Gaynor found for us in Brazil. The original angel is dressed in blue robes; the other colors were taken from the curtain fabric in the living room where we use the pillows.

26—All the angels are done in petit point. On just this one

I experimented with threads of gold to recreate the gilt that still remains on the wings of the original figure.

27—The ostrich feathers on the tiny pillow on the following page came from an early Wedgewood design. The pillow stays always on the small French slipper chair on page 95.

last. It is, you are free to say, strange that no two faces are the same. This is not for lack of trying. In fact, I was also determined that all four faces would look exactly like the original—only to find with each finished angel that it could not be closer than a second or third cousin, once removed. By the time I was on the third, I told myself that my technique was no doubt faulty. But I probably could not have made them identical by any method but plotting the stitches first on a graph. I think I enjoyed far more trying to recapture our angel in petit point by trail and error as I did.

As I was about to start the fourth and last, I remembered that I had meant to do all the wings with gold thread, which I had never used before. The fourth, with the chartreuse background, not only has gold in the wings, but beyond the edge of the picture of it is a not very brilliant gold star. I have seen well-meaning friends pick the pillow up and flick the star with their fingers, thinking it a temporary spot of dirt. I quickly look away and out the glass doors up into the star-studded sky, and I see no "spot" on the pillow—to me it is a glittering star made with shimmering gold thread.

No, I never gave a thought to taking out and re-doing the other wings with gold. I have seen experts using threads of gold with the greatest of ease, achieving glorious golden designs. I have bought a half dozen different kinds of gold thread especially made in as many countries for needlework, and I have yet to work any of them with any ease whatsoever. I have made a date in one of the years ahead to take the time to go to an expert and learn before using one more gold thread for another angel's wing, or a star, or any golden thing again.

28 & 29–On the preceding page, the famous "Chessy" asleep in a fanciful Pullman berth, a gift to Walter Tuohy, president of the Chesapeake & Ohio Railroad and our generous host on many trips to Cleveland (page 88); and the Hallmark lion, a gift to Joyce C. Hall, president of Hallmark Cards, who has so often made his home our home in Kansas City (page 89).

30–Opposite, rose taken from a French horticultural print by Redouté, a gift to our friend, a great lover of plants, and my long-time director, Gower Champion; in his plant room in California (page 90).

ENGSTEAD

The ostrich-feather pillow

Some say the reason needlepoint is fascinating to do is that it is "creative." I shy away from that word; it is too self-conscious to apply to a small needlepoint pillow. I am sure a better description is just the plain, small word, "fun." The story of the ostrich-feather pillow in color picture 27 explains what I mean.

We have always loved Wedgwood porcelain, used it at breakfast, lunch, and dinner, and have, from time to time picked up pieces in New York, London, Brighton, and San Francisco. In 1952, when we were in London, the four of us, Larry, Heller, Richard, and I visited the Wedgwood factory, where we were shown how to make our own pair of black basalt vases. It was there, too, that at long last we saw the complete Wedgwood dinner service we had always hoped to find and we have used it with genuine pleasure ever since.

Shortly thereafter, in a London antique shop, we were attracted to what appeared to be a French porcelain plaque. To our delight, we discovered that it was a very early piece made at the Wedgwood factory when Josiah Wedgwood was still experimenting with the style of design for which he was to become so famous. He imported French and Italian painters to create for him what they considered the ideal designs and patterns for the period. And here we had found one of these early samples, a lady with an ostrich-plume headdress painted, as we had suspected, by a French artist. Heller had her own ideas about the lady. She insisted that the painter must have been awfully homesick in England. "He must have been thinking of his mother—she's so *old*!" she said.

Three years later, I went to Paris with Helen Hayes and George Abbot to appear in *Skin of Our Teeth*, and of course Richard and I went window shopping and of course we saw something I immediately wanted to put under my arm and take away—for Heller's room in our house in Connecticut—a tiny French slipper settee. When we got it home, it seemed naturally to belong with the "French" Wedgwood plaque, but we agreed a third something was needed. Needlepoint. A pillow. Spontaneously, somebody said, "The Old Mother's ostrich plumes!"

Since then, the plaque, the chair, and the pillow have been in quite a few rooms, but they have always been together. It was fun to have an idea connected with the Wedgwood that had so long been an interest of ours, to make our own design (right or wrong, good or bad—we do think there is a flaw), and it has been fun to live with them and move them from room to room as circumstances changed and always to find them exactly right together. You can call this creative if you will, but it is not really so complicated as that—it is simply fun.

....

The only thing I added to the enlarged sketch of the ostrich plumes on this canvas was a circle of a narrow repeat design taken from the one that surrounds the figure of the Old Mother on the plaque, for the plumes looked somewhat disembodied alone on the pillow. Later, in fact, several years later, I realized that the circle would have been much better if I had done it in greater detail in petit point. The same thing happened another time when I did a repeat motif for a circle around our hydrangea design (color picture 10).

I offer two bits of advice as a result. First, even if you are not sure you will want to do petit point on a canvas, use a double canvas anyway, just in case it turns out that you do need to split the mesh for petit point. If you like single canvas, as I do, because it is white and somehow prettier to work on than the usual beige linen of double canvas, well,

white double canvas is now becoming quite generally available at last. Second, it is very likely that a small repeat motif done in a *circle* will have to be done in petit point to make the detail come out right all the way around. This is basically because the rows of stitches on a canvas line up with the mesh itself, vertically and horizontally, plus, in a choppy sort of way, diagonally (you come to understand this when you learn the basketweave stitch, page 138). In the usual ten-, twelve-, or even fourteen-stitch needlepoint canvases, it is difficult to make a small design go around a curve evenly unless you work it in proportionately smaller petit-point stitches.

If you don't want to get into this, then make such borders straight-sided squares or oblongs, which cooperate with the direction of the canvas mesh. For example, the square bamboo frames in our dining-room rug (pages 72 and 73) could not have been easier to do. But the very simple scheme of horizontal and vertical light and dark lines would never have projected the bamboo effect if we had wanted to bend them into circles. It could be done, but not in the coarse stitch of single rug canvas; in the same narrow width, the curved bamboo would have to be drawn on double-mesh canvas and worked in petit point by splitting the mesh—or else drawn on a very fine canvas in the first place.

So, I should have done the ostrich-feather border differently, but I have never regretted such mistakes very much. It is fun to learn from experience, too.

On the
road

I love to go on the road. Many performers don't, for very good reasons. It is certainly not the easiest nor the most comfortable way to be in the theatre, but nevertheless I could write pages and pages on the satisfactions of performing on tour. There isn't room for that here, but among the needlepoint pillows I have done there are three that have to do particularly with my going on tour and the wonderful generosity of people who have made it easier and more comfortable for me.

They really did much more than that. Once, long ago, I said to Richard that I would liked to have lived in Lillian Russell's day. I remember very well the dubious look on his face when I said it, but he knew what I meant—the glamor, the opulence of that gilded age are gone forever. There will never be anything like it again. Or will there?

Long after, when we were touring in *One Touch of Venus*, we arrived in Cleveland one night with time only to leave our bags at a hotel and rush to the theatre. After the curtain came down, a most unexpected limousine and chauffeur were waiting to take us, not back to the hotel, but to the most comfortable and also one of the most magnificent apartments I had ever seen. It was in a most unexpected place, too—the railroad station! At the very top of the Terminal Tower of the Chesapeake & Ohio Railroad. The tremendous paneled living room was three stories high, way up in the sky looking over the whole city, and it had a pipe organ and two concert grand pianos. There were two dining rooms and a cozy breakfast room, and a stainless-steel kitchen. Our bedrooms were equipped with everything thoughtfulness could imagine to make us comfortable, including our luggage which had been spirited away from the hotel. There were flowers and bowls of fresh fruit, and my bathroom was *all* marble. And all of this was just for us. Richard looked at me and said, "So you would like to have lived in Lillian Russell's day!"

That was the first time, that was the way we met Walter Tuohy, then the president of the Chesapeake & Ohio Railroad, and his dear wife, who was also named Mary. It was only the beginning of our knowing them and their endlessly generous hospitality. In time, I was able to give them my small thanks in needlepoint, the pillow (color picture 28) of the famous "Chessy" asleep in a Chesapeake & Ohio Pullman berth—certainly the most comfortable kitten in history, but no more so than we were in our haven in the Tower.

In Kansas City I did something unforgivable. I referred to the city out loud, so people heard me, as Kansas City, Kansas! But we were in the other city, Kansas City, *Missouri*—only across the river, but you have no idea how unthinking the mistake sounds until you make it in a roomful of enthusiastic, hospitable people from Kansas City, Missouri. However, I must have been forgiven, for we have always been made to feel so very much at home on our many return trips. And home was first of all the apartment of Joyce C. Hall, founder and president of Hallmark Cards of Kansas City, *Missouri*. The apartment had a wonderful view overlooking the park. The walls were covered with his collection of paintings by famous artists from countries all over the world, from Dali to Grandma Moses. Above all, he made us feel this was truly our own home.

And then there was the cook, who made such heavenly baking-powder biscuits, fried chicken, cream gravy, pancakes with sausage fresh from the Halls' farm. Of course, the chickens and milk and cream and butter came from the farm, too. Everyone has heard how well Lillian Russell and Diamond Jim Brady ate at Delmonico's—but Delmonico's wouldn't even know how to do anything to compare with this.

One Sunday morning, I awoke at an early hour (early for me, eleven o'clock) to be greeted by a scene like a Christmas card, the park outside blanketed with snow. Immediately—almost immediately, after a breakfast of pancakes and ham from the farm, popovers, fresh butter, homemade strawberry jam, two huge cups of coffee—I started a painting of the park in the snow, hoping it would in some way convey to our kind host what his home meant to us. It snowed all day, and I painted all day, until dark. But it didn't work out. The trouble is, I am a realist when I paint. I started with a feathery white canvas in the morning, and then I looked so hard at that view trying to capture it that as the day got darker and darker, so did the painting, until my snow scene was almost black. Richard didn't seem to think this makes as much sense as I think it does, but in any case we never told Joyce Hall about the realistic painter who tried to give him a painting. Later I sent him the needlepoint pillow of the lion hallmark with crowns representing the emblem of Hallmark Cards (color picture 29). It's not a painting, but with needlepoint I do seem to be on safer ground sometimes.

Some years later, on tour again, there was a change of address in Kansas City and we stayed in the beautiful modern apartment Alexander Girard had designed for visiting friends of Joyce Hall at the very top of the high, high Hallmark factory, with great plate-glass windows overlooking *both* Kansas City, Missouri, *and* Kansas City, Kansas. But nothing had really changed. Fried chicken was cooking and gay greetings of welcome-back awaited us to make us feel once again that all was right with the world back home in Kansas City. And when we saw Joyce Hall's handsome new office, he had placed there only two personal items, the little lion pillow on his couch and a large oil landscape by Sir Winston Churchill above the fireplace. I was *indeed* truly flattered!

The last time I saw the rose pillow I gave to Gower Champion, we were on the road again, in California, in *I Do!*

I Do! which he directed. As an actress who likes to tour, I certainly owe Gower Champion special thanks of some sort, for he also directed *Hello, Dolly!* in which we went on an international tour that took us to Okinawa, Tokyo, Kyoto, Korea, Vietnam, Hong Kong, Bombay, Bangkok, Beirut, and back to London again. That was no ordinary experience, nor could it have happened "in Lillian Russell's day."

I had made the pillow some time before, and we had chosen the rose for Gower Champion because more than anyone I have ever known he loves plants and flowers of all kinds. His knowledge and appreciation of everything that grows up through the earth is a joy to see and in some way touches everything he does. I remember a conversation I had with him about three mutual projects, the tour of *Hello, Dolly!*, a spring television show, and the production of *I Do! I Do!* that would come later. As we went through the itinerary for "*Dolly*," I realized that with each country that was named, sooner or later Gower would speak of the native plants and flowers of special beauty that we would see there. In both the television show and in one of the big musical numbers in *I Do! I Do!*, masses of flowers on the sets were to be the key that would first tell the audience what he wanted to project.

We were in Brazil when this conversation took place, walking along the main drive at the farm. Gower stopped without warning as I walked ahead, talking to the air. When I realized he was no longer beside me and turned back, I saw him gazing at a large acreage we had recently planted with young eucalyptus trees. Gower knows everything about root systems, soils, the planting and care of living things and how they will grow. He was standing there, oblivious to everything else, thinking, with pleasure I could literally see in his eyes, of how that grove of eucalyptus would grow and flourish for years to come.

I know nothing of root systems and soils, but for Gower Champion I knew that any needlepoint I might do would be of flowers as nearly true to life as could be managed. It only took a slight dare from Richard to try a rendering in petit point of this oversize rose taken from a portfolio of famous horticultural prints by the French artist Redouté. I was pleased when I first saw the finished pillow in the Champions' New York living room but even more so when I saw that Marge Champion had brought it with them to their California home. It was photographed (color picture 30) in their glass-enclosed plant room, high up in the hills, from where we could see Los Angeles, Hollywood, Beverly Hills, and the Pacific Ocean. All around it were Gower's plants, flourishing under his admiring, understanding touch. And I paused to think that he directs actors, actresses, singers, and dancers, too, with very similar results.

....

Different as these three pillows are from each other, the designing of all three had something in common. To be effective, the needlepoint had to render the designs accurately, so I took no chances and had them painted on the canvases for me. The oversize Hallmark lion is the simplest and a moderately skilled amateur could have traced this on canvas from a good photostat. I was able to stitch it all in needlepoint, without resorting to petit point. "Chessy" came, of course, from an old Chesapeake & Ohio advertisement and the kitten is in petit point.

The Redouté rose was blown up by photostat to a larger size than the original print. It is important to understand why this was necessary, because "realistic" needlepoint can get you into all kinds of trouble. Trying to do too much detail in too small a space simply does not work and the results will look fussy and awkward. In the larger version of the rose, there was room to render the more important horticultural details, so that at a distance it looks remarkably "real." But close to, you can see the details are really simplified and rendered in a way that does not push the needlepoint beyond what it can legitimately do. And even so, there was no question but that the rose had to be done in petit point.

Pillows
and chairs

Some chairs seem to speak right up and ask for pillows or seat cushions. And no avid needlepointer will use a plain pillow for long where a needlepoint pillow might do better! For chairs that are of themselves interesting pieces of furniture, I like quiet, formal designs, and yet, in this group of six of our favorite chairs on the following pages, two have pillows that are quite different.

The first chair on the left is Richard's desk chair. I had noticed he seemed to find it more comfortable with a pillow tucked in it, so I made this one as a surprise gift when he opened his Hallmar (Hall for Halliday, Mar for Martin) offices. The design is white lilies-of-the-valley on a soft orange background. The flowers represent the wedding bouquet that I never had when we ran away (happily telling our families all about it) to get married. We have always agreed these are the flowers I would have carried if we had had a church wedding.

The next chair is French and the formal monogram "M" on the seat cushion is taken from the Aubusson tapestry that is now in our bedroom (page 67). The wreath of flowers is yellow mimosa. It is a painted chair—tones of soft blue-green—and the upholstery is pale gold-beige velvet. All very discreet and muted and pretty to look at by the grand piano in the living room where we presently have it.

The little bamboo-turned high chair was a Christmas gift from Nancy and Leland Hayward. Nancy has an eye for

93

the different and the decorative and her chair has been a charming ornament in the several rooms where we have used it. It is hardly big enough to sit on, which was a great advantage the day that I carried it bodily, along with the twenty-six needlepoint squares of our dining-room rug, to Mazaltov's needlepoint shop to have the bamboo turnings in the back of the chair translated into a needlepoint motif to frame those squares. (That complicated story starts on page 71.) The chair does not really need a cushion, but since I had a small, round needlepoint pillow, it was irresistible to set it on the chair's small, round seat.

The wing chair covered with black-and-white French *toile* comes from Richard's study. The oblong pillow is a perfect fit in the deep recess of this large chair and makes it much more comfortable. This pillow I did not make. Richard and I bought it in England, one of several Victorian needlepoint pieces we found that intrigued us (another being the valence of similar design that is also in his study, shown on page 26). If you wonder why the design of the pillow stands out so boldly against the already bold pattern of the *toile*, that is because the pillow is beaded. All the clear, modeled forms are achieved with dozens, hundreds, of beads slipped one at a time into the needlepoint stitches. I am determined I will learn how to do this someday.

The fifth chair is the French slipper settee Richard and I saw while we were window shopping in Paris a good many years ago. It is even smaller and lower than you would think from the picture and was a perfect, romantic child's chair; we put it first in Heller's room when we had the house in Connecticut. The tiny pillow with the curl of ostrich feathers has been sitting in the chair for years, and both are now in Richard's study. It is one of our favorite needlepoint fantasies, derived from the Wedgwood design which we treasure described on page 85.

The last chair is my dressing-table stool. It is an old weaver's stool, still painted a worn greenish-blue, which we bought in an antique shop in Danbury, Connecticut. At the same time, we bought an apothecary's chest made of bleached pine—shallow, high, and wide, with twenty-six drawers—that has been my dressing table ever since. I seem to be forever unsuccessful in convincing anyone that I really do prefer to perch on this high stool than to use a conventional dressing-table chair, but both these pieces of furniture have seemed exactly right to me for all the twenty-five years I have been using them. Fifteen years ago, I chose a wreath of blue forget-me-nots with slender green leaves for the pale blue-green velvet seat cushion, for wherever we have built, bought, or rented, we have always used shades of blue for our bedroom.

Presents from dear friends

Dorothy Hammerstein makes me believe in the chemistry of people. From the first moment I met her, I knew she would always delight me. She has a wonderful sense of humor and I always laugh a lot when I am with her for we see people and things in such a similar light. There is even a piece of needlepoint that proves how much we can think alike.

Way back in the fall of 1939, I visited Jerome Kern in his Beverly Hills home. This dear man, this pixie, this heavenly talent of melody, had a way of bringing out the fun in everyone and he loved to take the time for a good visit. We spent the afternoon in his sun-filled music room playing the piano and singing. I felt as though I was in the treasure house of the richest man in the world as he showed me all his gold and jewels, all made of pure music. He reached in his files and pulled out sheets and sheets of music covered with penciled notes. He would sit hurriedly at the piano and play only a bar or phrase, a chorus or verse of some of them— songs he had written but never published—and then get up to find still more to play. There was one he played three times which was later published as "Long Ago and Far Away." Another he repeated even more times because he saw I liked the lyrics. One line is, "Here's the sweetest sight that I have seen . . ."

Twenty years later, I learned that Dorothy Hammerstein—who was several thousand miles away the day I sang that song over and over with Jerome Kern in California— that Dorothy had just about then been finishing a needlepoint

I HAVE SEEN A LINE OF SNOW WHITE BIRDS
DRAWN ACROSS AN EVENING SKY.

I HAVE SEEN DIVINE, UNSPOKEN WORDS
SHINING IN A LOVER'S EYE.

I HAVE SEEN MOONLIGHT ON A MOUNTAIN TOP
SILVER AND COOL AND STILL.

I HAVE HEARD CHURCH BELLS FAINTLY ECHOING
OVER A DISTANT HILL.

CLOSE ENOUGH TO BEAUTY I HAVE BEEN
AND, IN ALL THE WHOLE WIDE LAND,

HERE'S THE SWEETEST SIGHT THAT I HAVE SEEN—
ONE OLD COUPLE, WALKING HAND IN HAND.

WORDS BY O.H.

OCTOBER
1939   STITCHED BY HIS LOVING WIFE D.H.

31–*Petit-point bag, a present to myself (page 109).*

32–*Leaf pillow, a gift from Dorothy Hammerstein.*

piece of those very lyrics, by Oscar Hammerstein. There is the evidence below the verse: "Words by O. H.—October 1939—Stitched by his loving wife D. H." The night I appeared for the last time as Maria in *The Sound of Music,* I was especially touched by the gift I found waiting for me when I returned home—Dorothy's precious needlepoint verse.

On another, very different kind of day—not a day of celebration, a birthday, nor opening or closing of a show day, but on an average kind of day—another needlepoint present arrived from Dorothy, sent because she simply wanted to send it. It was her leaf pillow (color picture 32, opposite) which, wherever we are, we have since always had in a room that we use a majority of the time. Its handsome, clean design adapts gracefully wherever we put it, and I admire it with a needlepointer's eye, too, for Dorothy works with an exceptionally lovely, even stitch.

And another present. Christmas, 1968. For more than half a year, Robert Preston ("Michael") and I ("Agnes") had been touring in *I Do! I Do!* Richard was with us and so was Robert's wife, Catherine. People often ask, "What does the wife of a star *do* during those long trips?" On Christmas morning we opened a shining gold box containing just one of the many lovely things Cathy does while we are all traveling, the brilliant yellow wool pillow cover in color picture 34, worked with her own design in lace appliqué, wool crewel, and needlepoint.

With it came a note about the quotation in needlepoint, which is from a book by the poet, May Sarton. It said: "Dearest Mary and Richard . . . When we came across this quotation from *Plant Dreaming Deep,* we felt it should be preserved in some way for you. Not that you need the admonition, but because you both so exemplify the truth of the thought . . . with our very special love, Cathy and Robert." This is praise perhaps I should not repeat, but I do

100

31

32

33

34

IT IS GOOD
FOR A PROFESSIONAL
TO BE REMINDED THAT
HIS PROFESSIONALISM
IS ONLY A HUSK,
THAT THE REAL PERSON
MUST REMAIN AN AMATEUR,
A LOVER OF THE WORK.

CP

anyway because I feel so strongly about the truth of the thought in the quotation Cathy and Robert chose:

"It is good for a professional to be reminded that his professionalism is only a husk, that the real person must remain an amateur, a lover of the work."

We first knew Cathy as an actress thirty years ago when she was under contract to Paramount Pictures and Robert and I were doing a motion picture, *New York Town*, for the same company. They were married the same year Richard and I were. They are very old friends indeed and closer than ever since we have done *I Do! I Do!* together—rehearsals, three months of Broadway tryouts, a year's run in New York, and especially those months on tour. I don't know how Cathy managed not to let us suspect she was making the pillow cover, which she began in the early weeks of the tour, but she did surprise us completely. We have taken it to Brazil where it has been placed on the large bed in the yellow-and-white bedroom of the guest house. I cannot resist, I am planning to adapt the design for small needlepoint pillows to go with Cathy's big one.

And, people may ask, "What does a star's *husband* do with his time on tour?" Richard has so much to do I can't keep track, but just one small thing was to rush the pillow cover air-mail, special-delivery to New York to be photographed at the eleventh hour for this book.

Cross-stitch alphabet
sampler, dated 1821; a gift
from Joshua and Nedda
Logan.

The samplers

On either side of our elevator door in the New York apartment are two framed pieces of needlework that are also presents from thoughtful friends. They must have a fascinating history, but we know only very recent bits of it.

One day in 1955, a package was delivered and I recall vividly the moment when I had unwrapped the brown paper and the tissue paper and saw the words before me—MARY MARTIN HER WORK 1821. It's true that by 1955 I had become fairly well accustomed to seeing my name in unexpected places, but in needlework dated well over a century earlier, it was startling. There is nothing that someone, somewhere, sometime hasn't thought of before—not even one's very own name!

The sampler was handsomely presented in an antique gold frame, with a brown velvet mat at the top of which was a pair of clasped hands, perhaps the most thoughtful touch of all. There was a note that said, "With love from Josh and Nedda Logan," followed by a rather long explanation. The Logans had been driving through New England and as they sped through the countryside in New Hampshire, they came to a road blocked off by police and firemen. Not far beyond, a lovely old house was in flames. The frantic owners were getting some of their possessions out through a second-story window. Nedda and Josh left their car and watched in concern, and as they moved closer they saw a framed picture that had fallen to the ground, face down and smoking. Josh went to turn it over and put out the smouldering spot under

Dear Parents I am young and cannot show
such work as I unto your goodness owe
Be pleased to smile on this my best endeavour
I'll strive to learn and be obedient ever

Mary Martin
Her Work
1839

the broken glass. The charred place still shows in the lower left-hand corner. And then he saw the name and the date. I feel as though I had been there with them, I can see so vividly the Logans dismayed by the painful sight of a home being destroyed and holding this old piece of needlework that would be such a delightful surprise for me. In spite of all the confusion, they were able to buy it a little later.

Some years afterwards, I had a similar surprise. This time, when I undid the wrappings I saw—MARY MARTIN HER WORK 1839—and it was Katharine Cornell and Nancy Hamilton who had found another sampler for me in Nantucket. Surely it must be by the same Mary Martin, the style is so very much the same even though the motifs are somewhat different. Did she move to Nantucket, I wonder, and why do her two cats look so bitterly sad in the new environment?

And then, ten years after that, Richard and I flew to the remote island of Eleuthera for a five-day rest at the Potlatch Club before I started rehearsals for *Hello, Dolly!* It is a comfortable, congenial place and as soon as we arrived we went out to explore the beautiful beach nearby. When we got back to our rooms, just inside our front door stood a tiny table with a large card on it that read, "Welcome to Mary Martin from Mary Martin."

The top of the table is a molding around glass that covers another sampler signed—MARY MARTIN JUNE 4 1800. This much earlier work *must* be by the same Mary who did the sampler of 1839. There is the very same tree in the Garden of Eden, laden with apples, complete with serpent, Adam, and Eve, with somewhat less expert versions of the floral motifs in the later piece. Mary Martin was already quite a proficient needlewoman in 1800, but she was still having trouble with her letters. I wonder if people worried about how she was doing in school, the way people used to worry about me. I was never known as a good student and everyone (except me) worried from the first to the last day that I went to school. How old could this Mary have been when she was set to stitching the very solemn and illegible motto at the bottom of her sampler, dating it with the "J" in "June" backside-to? It says:

> Favour is deceitful and beauty
> is vaine, but a woman that feare
> th the Lor [Lord?], she shall be praised

It is a tiny sampler, just big enough under its glass top to hold Richard's telephone which he likes to keep off his desk in his study. To add to the mystery of who Mary Martin could have been and where she really lived, the owner of the inn on Eleuthera who gave us the little table said she had found that sampler not in the United States but in the northern part of England.

. . . .

Of course, the three nineteenth-century Mary Martin samplers are not needlepoint. They are cross-stitch on linen, one of the many versions of what is called counted-thread embroidery. But, especially in the filled-in shapes of the designs, this old cross-stitch is very like needlepoint. There is, in fact, a needlepoint version of cross-stitch done on canvas—two stitches made over each other but in opposite directions to

106

form an "x." (I used it on the canvas for the purple evening purse in color picture 35; the method, on page 116, is not quite the same as for embroidery cross-stitch.) Just about any of these old cross-stitch motifs could be translated into single-stitch needlepoint designs, especially the decorative borders.

The important differences between the two kinds of needlework are these: On the cross-stitch samplers, the backgrounds are not filled in; and, the foundation is not open-weave canvas (page 127), on which stitches line up almost automatically, but a linen cloth, not tightly woven but fine nevertheless, on which the threads must be carefully counted in order to place the stitches evenly. The scale of stitches on linen is that of fine petit point. In the past, petit point was indeed often done on linen rather than on needlepoint canvas.

By more careful counting, you can make stitches of two

sizes on linen, the equivalent of fine needlepoint and extra-fine petit point. This is what I did on a piece of modern embroidery linen for my own "sampler" of theatre motifs shown nearly life-size in color picture 36. This is not something recommended for beginners, but having become used to petit point I did not find it hard, just time-consuming. I used on the soft linen equally soft cotton embroidery floss. Even fine wool strands would be rough and irregular for such fine stitches on the close linen weave.

But the extra-fine petit point did lead to an unforeseen hazard. When I first started the "Theatre Sampler," I worked by an open window in hot California sunshine and I used a magnifying glass to check stitches in the tiny details. One day, I left the magnifying glass on the canvas in the sun, and, yes, it actually burned. A large ragged hole with scorched edges had eaten into both linen and stitches and I had to start all over again on a new piece of linen.

Some small
gifts for others

Many times, I have said, "Coral is my favorite color—or shrimp." But then, I've also said jonquil yellow and French blue and beige and brown. Valentina once designed a suit for me which she insisted was a lovely elephant grey. The image of a lumbering grey elephant didn't seem lovely to me, but I wore that suit for years because *I* felt it was my favorite rich shade of brown. Favorite colors remind me of the moments in the theatre when a performer is asked, "What is your favorite role?" The standard answer is, "The one I'm playing." I am guilty of saying the same thing, though I may very well mean it at the time. However, an embarrassed laugh usually follows and the interviewer smiles politely as he asks, "But I mean really?"

So the answer to which is my favorite color will sometimes be quite truthfully, "The one I'm wearing," coral, for over the years I've been more and more attracted to many different shades of coral-colored fabrics, especially for summer dresses. Since I have never found a bag of a good coral color, I decided to make one myself, the one in color picture 31, to carry with coral-and-green summer dresses, or with white dresses with a coral or green scarf.

This is the only piece of needlepoint I have ever made entirely for myself. Small as it is, somehow it seemed to take as long to finish as the largest rug I've ever done (maybe it *did* take as long?). It was a subtle lesson in the old truth, "It is better to give than to receive." Favorite color or not, working on the coral bag lacked the chief joy of doing needlepoint, the pleasure of thinking as one works of the person it is for. This, alas, was only a present for me. I'm actually very pleased with it, but I liked so much better doing the small gifts for others in this chapter.

The leaf design was an experiment and a rehearsal for something else as well. I've long hoped to do a rug of leaves of every possible shade of green, but I wanted to try them on something smaller first. I learned with these greens that a pale color, here shrimp rather than coral, would be the better background, leaving the ladybug, the end pieces, and the frame to be the strongly "coral" elements of the finished bag. (The gold handle has pieces of real coral set in it. It is from Thailand, though we bought it in Hong Kong.)

This was also the first time I experimented with combining cotton and wool in the same design. I wanted the background and the leaves to have different textures, but at the time I couldn't find silk in the shades of green I wanted. I found the right colors in the same kind of rich, silky looking cotton embroidery floss that I used for the summer pillows in the living room. It worked very well on the fine petit-point canvas that I used here (page 131). The floss had to be split for the fine canvas, just as wool is split for petit point.

When my sister-in-law Didi and her husband Whit were building their new home in Connecticut, I hoped that if I did a petit-point portrait of the house and had it made up as an eyeglass case, Didi would enjoy using it—and would stop running all over New Canaan and the surrounding country-side asking, "Did I leave my glasses?" Have you seen my glasses? Are you sure you haven't?" I was also optimistic that people would recognize the house on the case and would phone, "Don't worry, we've got your glasses case and the glasses are in it."

We arranged to have the present waiting at the house the

110

day they moved, and we couldn't wait to visit on housewarming day. There, on the wall in the front hall, was Didi's eyeglass case, framed exactly as it is in the photograph. "Of course," Didi said, "Took it downtown to be framed the minute I saw it. Wouldn't think of losing it. Love it there!"

Didi is still going around losing her glasses. But I am grateful to her; I didn't solve her problem, but she gave me two ideas in place of one. It is easy and fun to do petit point this size, a little portrait of a house is one design that seems to ask to be framed, and it is a housewarming present for everybody in the family. On a different occasion, I'll try again for someone the self-returning (I hope) eyeglass case.

111

My son Larry's and his wife Maj's fifth anniversary was the occasion for the clasped-hands design in color picture 33, for our children have become fond of our family symbol, too. Freda Bachrach, the wife of our dear family doctor, David, first worked this quaint, simple version of friendship hands as a present for us and let me copy it. That was ten years ago, and I felt a warm glow of pleasure when only recently, when we went to visit Larry and Maj and their children, I saw the pillow still sitting in the favorite comfortable chair of the master of the house.

· ·

With a design like the clasped hands, it is the subject itself that interests you and, as happened here, it may not be of a size and shape to make a pillow or other useful object. Still, it may not lend itself to framing either, which can be so thoroughly unsuccessful with most pieces of needlepoint. The solution here was to have the needlepoint piped in satin and then mounted on a larger, brown velvet pillow, a nice compromise that "frames" it but allows it to be used as a fabric as it should be.

· ·

I learned a great lesson which I want to share with every woman in the world. Never try secretly to do a piece of needlepoint as a surprise for your husband. This very small, imperfect, mixed-up example of petit point is shown here as proof of what I mean. It caused more anxiety, confusion, suspense, and fright than anything I have ever made.

And—do not try to do needlepoint in a closet, either with, let alone without, a light bulb. I tried it both ways. If you happen to be an actress, do not attempt to take "one last stitch" just before the curtain goes up or while you are waiting for a cue. Those smouldering little backstage lights may make you optimistic that you can see what you are doing, but as this result plainly shows, you are a cockeyed optimist.

Richard was leaving for a quick trip to Brazil—for the

first time without me. After the long trip alone, when he opened his suitcase I wanted him to find a surprise. I bought him a green silk sports jacket—bright green, just right to wear at the farm—and had the handkerchief pocket removed so I could replace it with a petit-point pocket. The design is a shield with our clasped hands, the name of the farm, and our initials. I still like the idea. The doing of it was torment.

After living with her husband for close to thirty years, a wife has a right to think she knows his daily pattern, his business and personal and social routine. It was a shock to learn this is not exactly true. It was frightening to think it was safe to relax and enjoy the fun of making a surprise for him, only to hear his familiar footsteps only half a hallway away, and he wasn't supposed to be anywhere around for at least two hours! It is very awkward to collect needles, wools, scissors, canvas, quickly push them under a seat cushion, and then to be found sitting twiddling your thumbs with a smile, for no reason, on your face. The run for the nearest closet, as I've said, is equally, obviously disastrous for the needlepoint, even if it keeps the secret.

I did keep the secret, but there is a better solution. Boldly bring out the needlepoint you plan to do for your husband and simply say, "Look, dear, I am making this as a surprise for you," and then proceed to stitch away in peace. The result will be, I guarantee, more successful than Richard's pocket.

Presents
for Jerry
and Didi

I loved making the pale-blue purse covered with flowers and fruits for my sister, Jerry, who has not been called Geraldine since the day after she was born. This needlepoint and I stayed close together and shared a memorable experience. I started it in Memphis, Tennessee, while I was touring the United States in *Hello, Dolly!* We made our way as far north as Vancouver, Canada, then south to San Francisco, and from there we flew by way of Honolulu to Japan, and I stitched and relaxed the whole way.

Looking at the purse now in color picture 35 brings back so many impressions of that trip—the fragrance of incense and tea in Tokyo, the smell of the sea and oysters near Kyoto where we went by the famous, fast express train. Together we faced dirt and filth and gunpowder in parts of Vietnam. There was the clean air of Okinawa, the red dust in Korea, the fragrances and smells and excitement of Hong Kong. I worked on it in Bangkok and Bombay—the less said about the heavy-filled air the better! In Beirut there was the clear mixture of sun and sea, and in Rome I even took the needle-point with me in a horse-drawn carriage.

"Dolly" settled down in London where I appeared at the Theatre Royal-Drury Lane for the third time, and I set a date to finish Jerry's purse by Christmas. And I did, with

time to spare to have it mounted on the gold and turquoise frame from India and sent to Texas in time for Christmas.

The other bag, the purple one, is for another sister. By law, she is my sister-in-law, but she has never been less than dearest Didi to me. As you can see from the background of purple silk in the picture, it is being made to carry with an unusually lovely Indian sari—and, as is plain to see, both the bag and the sari dress are still to be finished.

This, like every piece I have ever started, I began with great enthusiasm, but I soon found it had its own demanding personality. It requires complete relaxation, concentration, and most of all it is exacting about light—not too much, not too little, and at a certain height. On this, again, I have dared experiment with gold thread for the design, and again I don't find it easy. Only in the quiet of our farm in Brazil have I found it practical to work on this particular piece. I am looking forward to the lovely hours I will have to stitch on it there, for I am now able to set a date to finish it. By the time this picture of the one side I have done is published, we will have been on the farm for several months and I look forward to being able to wrap the completed bag with its jeweled clasp from India and to write the card . . . Merry Christmas, dearest Didi—1969.

The purple bag is stitched in cotton embroidery floss on double canvas. The mesh is split for petit point in the rosette designs. In order to get the purple thread to do justice to the sari silk, I found it necessary to do the background stitching twice, first with a dark purple thread, then with one just a shade lighter. With the darker thread, I first covered the background with the usual basketweave stitch (page 138). Then I turned the canvas around so that the next layer of lighter stitches would go in the opposite direction. This way, each finished stitch becomes a cross stitch; and this time, instead of doing the basketweave, I worked straight across each row in the Continental stitch (page 135). You can barely see that this is a two-tone stitch. What it does is to give the cotton floss an extra richness that really makes it look like silk.

116

DADDY

Mary Martin

The "Theatre Sampler"

One morning in San Francisco while we were touring in *I Do! I Do!*, I awoke from a dream in which I had seen myself paint little figures of past and present moments in shows that had meant the most to me. It was a lovely dream. Someone seemed to guide my hand as I painted the fur bonnet I wore and the trunk I sat on when I sang "My Heart Belongs to Daddy," the gilt "Venus" chair I sat on to sing "That's Him," and on and on all the way through to the fourposter in *I Do! I Do!* I really am not given to dreaming about needlepoint! Nevertheless, that very day I started the "Theatre Sampler" version of the dream painting. Could the other Mary Martin who did such beautiful samplers many years ago have anything to do with it? Even wide awake, I thought I sensed some encouraging advice coming from somewhere—"Go ahead, try your own, see what happens . . . ." What happened was that I had a great deal of fun with my "sampler," but I think I did not match the other Mary's fine workmanship.

The silk violet pillow (color picture 18) is shown "in progress" in miniature in the middle of the sampler. I was working on it here during the London run of South Pacific.

The fur bonnet and the trunk at the upper left belonged to "Dolly Winslow" who sang "My Heart Belongs to Daddy" in Leave It to Me.

With the help of Mainbocher, "Venus" in One Touch of Venus was very glamorous. Her gilt chair and chiffon scarf are at the upper right of the needlepoint.

The faithful wife in Lute Song wore a black headdress and played the lute; stitched in the middle at the left.

"Maria von Trapp" with the real Baroness von Trapp. Maria wore peasant costumes and played the guitar in The Sound of Music, *stitched in the center of the sampler.*

"Nellie Forbush" sat on a gasoline can and wore a straw hat (stitched in the middle at the right) when she sang "I'm in Love with a Wonderful Guy" in South Pacific.

Lower right, "Agnes" wore a marvellous feather- and lace-trimmed hat when she sang "Flaming Agnes" on the four-poster in I Do! I Do!

Lower left, petit-point Peter Pan sees his petit-point shadow!

119

The needlepoint rag doll, and then...

Among the many things I've learned about myself at Nossa Fazenda is that there I think of so many things to do, possibly too many, and that each one takes far more time than I expect. But that is what the farm is for. It is our place to "re-fuel," to get away from schedules, to think, to take the time to do the things there is no time for elsewhere. There I have at last taken the time to learn, more or less, to sew! Not really "all on my fingers," but, of all things, on an old-fashioned pedal sewing machine.

Shortly before leaving New York the last time, I saw an advertisement for a stuffed rag doll—an adorable nineteenth-century printed pattern of a Southern belle wearing a flowered dress, a muff, and a big hat tied with ribbons. It is made in just three pieces—front, back, and a circle for the base on which are printed the soles of two little shoes. I thought immediately what fun it would be to sew these up, fill them with the cotton we grow, and give them to the children of the families that live on the *fazenda*. I ordered also a tiny pattern for a Spanish lady wearing a mantilla.

Several weeks later at the farm, I had sewn one up and realized I would not want to make all the dolls alike. Why not paint my own, in oils on heavy cotton? Which I did, and it took three days. It was admired by both children and their parents and several adults who had no children even asked if they might have one too! I decided to do the next one with colored pencils, thinking it would go faster. It took two, almost three days. The next, I reasoned, would be faster done partly in oils for the face, the rest with appliquéd cloth of various colors for the muff, sash, and hat. That took four and one half days. I could see I was not keeping up with the heart-warming requests for rag dolls, when I thought of the idea that would *really* slow me up. It occurred to me that I wanted most of all to see what my Southern belle would look like in needlepoint. I quickly painted the doll on canvas in oils. That didn't take long because I only sketched the design in hastily, leaving the details to be worked carefully in the stitching—so, of course, I felt I was getting along very fast.

The needlepoint doll, as you can see, has only begun to take form and she has already taken not three or four days, but three or four weeks. But I am enjoying completely working on the sparsely outlined design, letting the stitches make the pattern come clear, using needlepoint or petit point as seems right as I go along. This needlepoint doll is in her way as much of a "rag" doll as the others; at any rate, she is made of leftovers—pieces of canvas that don't match which I found in Rio de Janiero and cotton embroidery floss that had accumulated during our travels in London, New York, and South America. She has been as much fun as anything I've ever tackled. Perhaps I've entered my second childhood!

I put her aside when we left the farm to go on the road with *I Do! I Do!*, having already paused to make two painted "boy" dolls—the Buckingham Palace Guard in his busby and the young Scotsman in kilts—for Heller's children. The Southern belle I will pick up soon and finish, I don't know exactly when or where nor even yet for whom. But I do know she will be an altogether gratifying accomplishment. She went on the road with me in the trunk that has one big drawer reserved for nothing but unfinished pieces of needlepoint. They are good traveling companions—restful, absorbing, fun, and yes, often sentimental! New ones, new ideas constantly join them and I hope always will. Some wait for the quiet of Brazil, others flourish any place, any time.

122

While we toured with I Do! I Do!, *the sewing machine at Nossa Fazenda waited over a year for me to get back to work and the children on the farm waited for more rag dolls.*

Perhaps, just as you have seen her, the unfinished needle-point doll and the other dolls explain a little what this book has been about. The pleasure of making something, of making a gift, of making it a certain way for a certain reason— for a special person, for a child, for a well-loved room. The pleasure of weaving together not just the threads and canvas of the needlepoint design, but also of weaving into the very stitches as you take them thoughts of people and places and living.

And so here I am, after all these years, making a doll! This is only the beginning!

123

Appendix

The Design

As I said at the start of this book, needlepoint is easy for beginners. There is only one stitch, though there are a number of ways to make it. Once you understand the stitch, you know the foundation of all the needlepoint you will ever do, no matter how complicated your projects become. And it is not at all an exaggeration to say that from the very first you can do needlepoint that looks far more difficult than it really is.

Needlepoint is "advanced" or "difficult" if you work a very intricate design very precisely in a great many colors, perhaps also with special realistic effects of shading. It is not the stitches but the *design* and how clearly it is indicated on the canvas that make a piece hard or easy to do. An experienced needlepointer may do the ultimate, a design worked freehand with little or no guidance at all drawn on the canvas. This *is* hard. I did it with the tiny hands in color picture 5 and I will do it again, but not often. More fun is the in-between method such as I used for the rag doll in color picture 37, where the design is indicated on the canvas very casually, showing only the general placement of colors and shapes and leaving the details to be worked out in the stitching. This is a little too much for a rank beginner, but someday it may become your favorite way to work.

My advice for a novice is: Choose first a design that is clearly painted in all its colors and detail on the canvas; and don't choose one that looks very involved and has dozens of colors and areas of shading. I have my word of warning about this, though. If the design is too simple, if it is just a collection of plain areas, *you are going to get bored*. Be brave, start with something that looks a little challenging if you want to have fun. Above all, choose something for a special purpose, for some more important reason than just "getting started on needlepoint."

124

Expert or inept, every needlepointer has to consider how to acquire the right design prepared in some form on the canvas, ready to stitch. I have tried just about all the possibilities. I have walked into Mazaltov's needlepoint shop in New York and other shops, seen ready-made designs I loved, bought them forthwith and rushed home immediately and started to stitch. Richard and I have worked out design ideas, found source material, made rough sketches, and had the pieces designed on canvas to order. This is the most extravagant way to proceed, and I must say it is fun. The most difficult-appearing design is amazingly easy if a professional has paved the way for you like this.

However, after a little experience, you begin to work pretty fast and the constant buying of prepared needlepoint designs becomes an investment. You may turn to designing your own out of financial desperation and, also, because of a nagging thought in the back of your mind that something *all* your own would somehow be more satisfactory than anything you can buy. This is true. It will happen, you will finally paint a design of your own on a blank canvas.

I will not try to tell you how to be a designer nor what to design. Everyone's skills and tastes are different. But there are some simple procedures for preparing a needlepoint canvas yourself that are a help to know and that will prevent a few disasters.

Get the complete design down on paper, in full color, to the size you want it. Even if you are expert at painting, make the design simpler than you would a painting; needlepoint can't and shouldn't render excessive realistic detail. If you are poor at drawing and painting, then trace, copy, paste together cut-outs, do anything you can think of to get around your lack of skill including, of course, sticking to a manageable design. But get it all down so you can see what it will look like and that you will like it.

Then, put a thin sheet of tracing paper over the whole thing and trace the outlines of all the shapes of the design, including outlines of important shadings of color within the main shapes (such as petals within a flower or gradations that render the modeling of a piece of fruit). Do this with a very black marking pen. What you are trying to achieve in the tracing is a diagram of where the colors belong.

Now, if the design is bold, or you would like it to be fairly primitive and undetailed, you can choose a canvas as coarse as ten stitches to the inch (see page 130). If the design is somewhat precise or detailed, 14-stitch-to-the-inch canvas is practical and the stitches will have a nice texture. A canvas any finer than that is no longer for a beginner, but the finer the canvas, the more detail you can do, someday. (Or, you can include some petit point, as I will explain later.)

You now retrace the black tracing onto the needlepoint canvas with an *absolutely waterproof* marking pen. You will find such pens in art-supply stores. Use grey or any medium tone, not black which will show through the stitches later. The way you know the pen is waterproof is to use it on a scrap of canvas, then wash the canvas under hot running water with soap and a nailbrush. The ink should not run nor blur. No less rigorous test will do, for the needlepoint will have to be washed and blocked when it is done, and if any markings under the stitches run even a little into the wool, the piece will be spoiled forever in a matter of instants, after all that work!

Once the outline tracing is on the canvas, it depends on you and the intricacy of the design whether you need color guidance on it too. The color sketch *might* be enough to tell you where the colors belong as you stitch, but the first time you should probably paint the colors into each area on the canvas before you start to work. Use either oil paints thinned with turpentine (thin enough, they will be stainproof) or with more water-proof colored marking pens (easier than paints). Now you will probably have a not very attractive version of your original design on the canvas. Don't get upset. Take your color sketch with you when you buy the wool, buy colors somewhat stronger, brighter, more contrasting than you think you need, and go home and start to stitch, fixing up your wobbly canvas design as you go along, using your sketch to remind you of what it is supposed to look like. All this will work. If your design does not attempt to be too realistic, the needlepoint version will actually be an improvement on the original sketch.

When you have been through this once, you will never quite recover. It is a wonderful feeling to have done it *all*. And after all these years, I have a very good idea of the economics of needlepoint. There is a small fortune to be saved in do-it-yourself design for a constant needlepointer.

The Canvas

There are two kinds of needlepoint canvas, single (or single-mesh, or mono) canvas and double (or double-mesh, or Penelope) canvas.

Single canvas is a comparatively modern innovation. It has an "open" weave with the threads wide apart, exactly like window screening. Each "mesh" or thread of the weave is a single thread. It is white and usually made of heavily starched cotton.

Double canvas is the traditional needlepoint canvas. It has the same open weave, but each "mesh" of the weave is a pair of parallel threads rather than a single thread. It is usually made of not so heavily starched natural-colored linen, though white cotton double canvas has recently become available.

The mesh size (or gauge) of canvas indicates how many threads (single or double) it has to the inch. Since one needlepoint stitch is made over every mesh, the mesh size automatically tells you how many stitches there will be in a 1-inch row. There are innumerable mesh sizes; some of the more common ones are 10, 12, and 14 stitches to the inch for needlepoint, 18 and 24 stitches to the inch for petit point.

Beginning on page 135, the instructions for making needlepoint stitches refer only to single canvas to make the process easier to explain. Each stitch is spoken of as being taken over "two crossed threads of canvas mesh," when, in fact, these two crossed threads would be two crossed *pairs* of threads in double canvas. It becomes complicated to say, over and over, that each thread of the mesh could be a double thread, but it is perfectly simple to understand when you have a double canvas before you (see next page), because each two threads of the pairs are placed close together in the weave so that you can *see* that they belong together and can be treated as one. Needle-

127

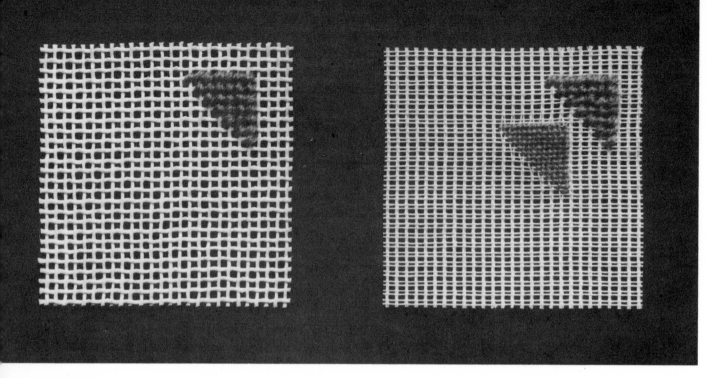

point stitches are made *exactly* the same way on double canvas as they are on single.

It is imperative to understand this. In fact, the best way to accept it is not to learn the stitches on single canvas at all, but to use double canvas to practice on in the first place. I learned on double canvas, on The Rug, without ever being aware that single canvas might be simpler. I never used single canvas until I happened to find in a shop a prepared design that I wanted that was painted on single canvas. I like single canvas; it is easy on the eyes and therefore a little faster to work.

But single canvas has a disadvantage that nothing can ever make up for. Only one size of stitch can be made on it. This means that if it is a coarse canvas, only one large size of stitch can be used. Or, if it is a very fine canvas, only one small size of stitch can be used, making even a small piece of needlepoint more laborious than it needs to be.

But on double canvas you can do both. What happens is this: Having mastered the idea that double canvas is worked by counting pairs of threads as single meshes, you now drop that thought entirely and look at all those paired threads, up, down, and sideways, as separate ones after all. You ignore that they are irregularly spaced to look like pairs (or push them around a bit with your needle so they are evenly spaced) and you will see that your fairly coarse double canvas—say 10 stitches to the inch—can now be looked at as being a fine *single* canvas of twice the number of stitches—20 to the inch. You then

128

proceed to work on it in tiny stitches that are otherwise in no way different in method from the larger needlepoint stitches you have learned. This is called "splitting the mesh," and you are doing petit point!

Petit point is no different and no harder than needlepoint; it is only smaller and slower. It may sound frightening, but it is not, and something wonderful happens to your design. The small, more intricate parts of it can be done in petit point to show more detail. Larger areas and the background can be done in faster needlepoint. And, the fineness of the petit point looks even better embedded in surrounding areas of coarser stitches than it would surrounded by more petit point. At least, this is often true; it depends on the nature of your design.

"Needlepoint" and "petit point" are merely comparative terms —one means larger, the other means smaller. You can do petit point without "splitting the mesh" of a canvas simply by using a very fine single canvas. Eighteen or even 16 stitches to the inch would qualify as petit point on single canvas. But be sure you really want to do the whole piece in so fine a stitch.

There are actual-size samples of needlepoint done on various canvases on the following pages. By referring to these and to the pictures of the finished pieces from which the samples were taken, you can get some idea of how much detail can be rendered on canvases of these mesh sizes. This is something to think about when you do your own designs or have them made to order. Don't put a detailed design on too coarse a canvas; don't waste time doing a simple design on a very fine canvas.

Also, another precaution when you choose a canvas: Your stitches, whether made of wool, cotton, or silk thread, must completely hide the mesh underneath. Therefore, you must test the thread on the canvas before you proceed. Wool is usually made of three loosely twisted strands and you can use all three or only one or two, or even add an extra strand. Cotton embroidery floss can also be thinned or thickened in the same way. Silk frays; use it as you buy it, on a very fine single canvas or to split the mesh of a double canvas for petit point. Rules about what thickness of thread will cover what mesh size of canvas are undependable. Test the thread yourself. The effect of the stitches should be plumply even—not lumpily packed, which would mean too heavy a strand; and not skinny and twisted, showing canvas behind, which would mean too thin a strand.

Rug canvas (single), 10
stitches to the inch worked
in wool. This is the
coarsest canvas you are
likely to use, but it does not
have to be used for rugs
only. It works up well
for large pillows and for
chair seats. The detail
is from the hydrangea rug
on page 32, and the design
is the "leaf" border Richard
designed originally for the
violet pillow in silk petit
point in color picture 18.
The same border from the
silk pillow is shown on
page 132.

Single canvas, 12 stitches to
the inch, worked in wool.
This a detail from one of
the hydrangea pillows in
color picture 10.
The 12-stitch mesh size
gives a prettier texture
than rug canvas for a pillow
which is seen close-to,
yet it is still fast to work. It
is often used for chair seats.

Single canvas, 24 stitches to
the inch, worked in silk.
This is a detail from the
bouquet of violets on the
pillow in color picture 18.
The silk stitching was a
pleasure and very, very
slow to do. All the
background is in the
same small stitch which, in
silk, is beautifully smooth. A
fine single strand of wool
could be used on the same
canvas, but the plain area of
background might not be as
even.

Single canvas, 14 stitches to the inch, worked in wool. This is a detail from a small pillow I did for our living room. The 14-stitch mesh size is ideal for many small projects, even as small as eyeglass cases. The stitch is delicate but not nearly as time consuming as petit point. It can usually be worked with only two strands of the usual 3-strand needlepoint wool.

Single canvas, 12 stitches to the inch, worked in cotton embroidery floss. This is a detail from a geranium pillow in color picture 2, made for our summer living room. The cotton covers the canvas, but it is not as heavy as wool and gives the effect of a smaller stitch, with a silky sheen. Cotton needlepoint is cooler to lean against than wool, and it is pleasanter to work on in hot weather, too.

Single canvas, 18 stitches to the inch, background worked in wool, leaves in cotton embroidery floss. This is a detail from the coral-colored petit-point pocketbook with green leaves in color picture 31. The 18-stitch mesh size is a good choice for a piece to be done all in petit point; the stitch is fine but takes considerably less time than working on 24-stitch canvas. Both the wool and the cotton were split into finer strands to fit this canvas.

Border of the silk violet pillow. Richard's repeat design for this stylized "leaf" border has proved wonderfully useful. It seems to work in any scale, 24 stitches to the inch here, only 10 to the inch in the hydrangea rug detail on page 130. Whatever canvas it is done on, the pattern itself is counted out with approximately the same number of stitches per "leaf."

Rug canvas (double), 10 stitches to the inch for needlepoint background, with mesh split 20 stitches to the inch for petit-point details; worked in wool. This is a petit-point rose from The Rug on page 8. The background is the same mesh size as the hydrangea rug detail on page 130. This is the piece on which I learned to do needlepoint, starting with a petit-point detail. With hindsight, I know that the design would never have worked if all the details had not been in petit point.

The Stitch

You may know that there are dozens of elaborate needlepoint stitches—that is, embroidery stitches that can be used on the open-weave canvases that are the foundation of the particular kind of needlework called needlepoint. Most books about needlepoint tell you about these "fancy" stitches, which go far back in the history of needlework. They give beautiful effects and are still very much in use in modern needlepoint design.

There is, however, one stitch which is *the* needlepoint stitch. The preceding photographs of finished stitching on various sizes of canvas mesh have shown what it looks like: It is plump and short, slants a bit from lower left to upper right, and lines up both vertically and horizontally on the canvas in closely packed rows. It is always the same, whether it is called needlepoint or petit point, because that distinction is only one of size.

There is one kind of needlepointer—I am one—who would rather achieve all the details of a design with this regular, endlessly repeated even texture of the one needlepoint stitch than any other, using the combination of needlepoint and petit point as the only variation. Perhaps laziness has something to do with not using the other stitches, but I have never thought so. The limitation of making the *colors* plus just the one stitch do everything is the challenge. There are even those who say that resorting to the fancy stitches is cheating. This is rather prejudiced, but I sympathise even if I don't agree.

So the instructions below are only for the one stitch—or for what appears to be just one stitch, for it is true that it has to be taken in several different ways. I use two ways, both well-known, plus a third way which has no formal name but which I know everybody uses. They are:

The Continental stitch (also called the Tent stitch): This is worked in horizontal rows along one mesh of the canvas at a time, from right to left. It is used for small areas only, as it tends to distort the canvas. It must never be used for backgrounds or large areas, as this pulls the canvas very badly out of shape.

The Basketweave stitch (also called the Diagonal Tent stitch): This is worked in straight rows, but the rows are diagonal, at a forty-five-degree angle. The diagonal is made up of a consecutive series of crossing-points of vertical and horizontal threads of the canvas. In the long run, the Basketweave is easier to use than the Continental, but it is harder to learn. It is always to be used for backgrounds and should be used in any comparatively large area.

Makeshift stitches: I have never seen anything written about these, but they happen constantly, and beginners need a rule for them. When you are doing either of the formal stitches in an area of color, the area has irregular edges; or, the design requires fitting just a few stitches of a color here and there. In both instances you then have to skip around to do what the design wants of you, and you loose track of whether you are doing the Continental or the Basketweave stitch. It makes no difference whatever which one you are doing in these little areas, and sometimes you may be doing neither.

What *is* important is the rule which applies to *all* needlepoint stitches, whether the two formal ones or my "makeshift" one: At *every* point on the canvas where a vertical and a horizontal thread of canvas cross, you always make a stitch which does this: *The wool comes up from behind the canvas in the square space at the lower left of the crossed threads; it goes over the crossing-point of the threads upward and to the right, and down into the square space at the upper right of the same crossed threads.* It then comes through to the front again via a square space that is at the lower left of another pair of crossed threads of canvas mesh *somewhere*—"somewhere" being simply the place nearest by where the design requires a stitch of the particular color you are using. Until you have practiced a few stitches, you will not understand what this means, but once you get going, keep that lower-left to upper-right rule always in mind, no matter what, and nothing that really matters can go wrong.

Since the rule applies to all the stitches, no matter how you mix your methods of stitching, the needlepoint comes out looking like all the same stitch on the front of the canvas. The only error worth getting upset about is when this doesn't happen. The stitches look different only on the back of the canvas.

134

"Makeshift" stitches look just that, makeshift; taken too far apart from each other, they can make loops (and bumps if you criss-cross around too much in back), but you can teach yourself to be neat with them. The Continental stitch makes even, horizontal rows of low-slanted stitches on the back. The Basket-weave makes a handsome, even weave that looks like perfect darning.

Do not try to understand the following practice instruction unless you have canvas, needle, and wool before you. They are simple, but you cannot visualize the results without the materials to work with.

To practice the Continental stitch: Draw a 1½-inch square in pencil on a scrap of single canvas, lining up the sides with horizontal and vertical meshes of the canvas. Thread a needle with wool and make a knot in the end of the wool. Insert the needle from the *front* of the canvas into the center of the pencil square, about 1 inch diagonally away from the upper-right-hand corner of the square. (That corner will be your real starting point.) Now pull the wool through until the knot holds in the canvas.

The upper-right-hand corner of the pencil square is made of two crossed threads of canvas mesh. Bring the needle and wool up from the back of the canvas into the empty space that is at the *lower left* of those two crossed threads. Now look 1) at this square space where the needle and wool came up. Look 2) at the empty square space that is at the *upper right* of the two crossed threads. And look 3) at the empty square space *directly to the left* of the one where the wool came up. Put the needle down into 2) and poke the tip of it up again through 3). Pull needle and wool all the way through. This is your corner stitch; don't pull it (or any stitch) too tight.

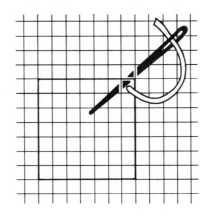

Now look at where the wool came up. This is 1) again, at the lower left of another pair of crossed threads of canvas. At the upper right is 2) again. Directly to the left of where the wool came up is 3) again. Put the tip of the needle down into 2) and poke it up through 3). Now stop and look at the position of the needle before you pull it all the way through. A needle in this slanting position will always make a true Continental stitch. Come back to this paragraph over and over until you are sure you see it. In addition, check that you see this: The previous (corner) stitch is on the right; the unfinished stitch is in the middle; and the needle poking up through 3) at the left is heading toward the beginning of the next stitch. The stitches are *accumulating* from right to left along one horizontal mesh of the canvas. But the finished stitches themselves on the canvas are *leaning* the opposite way, from left to right.

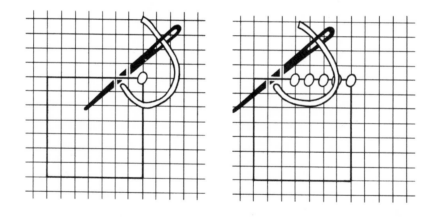

Keep going with the 1), 2) and 3) process to the end of the 1½ inches of the top of the pencil square. With the last stitch, put the needle through 2) to the back as usual, but *don't* poke it up through 3). Instead, turn the canvas around so that the last stitch you have made is at the *lower*-right-hand corner of the pencil square; in other words, turn the canvas upside-down.

Directly *above* the last stitch you made are two crossed threads of canvas mesh. Bring the needle and wool from the back of the canvas up through the empty square space that is at the lower left of those two crossed threads. You have a 1) again. Locate 2) and 3) again, and keep going along this new row, parallel and right next to the previous row, all the way to the end of the previous row. When you make the last stitch right above the end of the previous row, again leave the needle and wool at the back of the canvas when you go down into 2) and don't bring it up into a 3). Instead, turn the canvas upside-down again, so that the two row of stitches are back at the *top* of the pencil square.

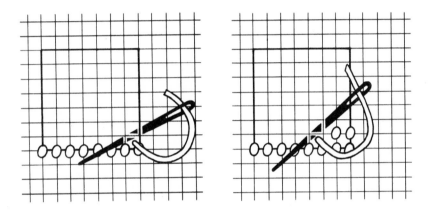

Directly *under* the last stitch of the second row is a pair of crossed threads of canvas mesh. The empty square space that is at the lower left of those crossed threads is your next 1). Find your 2) and 3), and by now you have learned the Continental stitch and are starting your third row. Keep going, 1), 2), 3), turning the canvas at the end of every row.

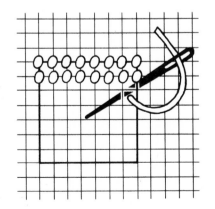

Eventually, the rows will accumulate until the stitches reach the knot that first held the end of the wool in place. *Always* cut the knot off before you stitch over that spot. The beginning of the wool is well trapped by now by the stitches that have been made over it.

You will find that the Continental stitch is the least confusing one to do, as a stitch, in the small areas of a design. But eventually, you will notice something: Turning the canvas around at the end of each row means that half the time you are looking at your design upside-down. This becomes annoying. The solution is to master the Basketweave stitch, which seems more involved at first, but for which you always keep the canvas right side up.

To practice the Basketweave stitch: On a scrap of single canvas, in pencil, draw the top and right sides of a 3-inch square. You don't need the rest of the square; just this upper right-hand corner of it is enough, and it *stays always* in the upper right. The pencil lines follow horizontal and vertical meshes of the canvas.

Thread a needle with wool and make a knot in the end of the wool. Insert the needle from the *front* of the canvas about 1½ inches away diagonally from the penciled corner. Pull the wool through until the knot holds in the canvas.

Instead of starting to stitch at the far corner, bring the needle and wool up to the front of the canvas through an empty square space along the top pencil line, about 1 inch to the left of the corner.

The space where the wool has come up is 1). It is located, as ever, at the lower left of a pair of crossed threads of canvas mesh. Put the tip of the needle down into the empty square space that is at the upper right 2) of the same pair of crossed threads. Now, in back of the canvas, head the tip of the needle *straight down vertically* under the first horizontal mesh of canvas it touches and under the next one below as well, and poke the tip of the needle up through to the front of the canvas. *Check*: The vertical needle went into 2); two horizontal threads of canvas mesh are lying across it, and these threads prove to be the top and bottom of an empty square space directly under 2) that the needle *skipped*; and, where the needle came up is 3), an empty square space directly under the skipped one. Look at this. It is the position of the needle that defines the first, *vertical* stage of the Basketweave process. Now pull the needle and wool through.

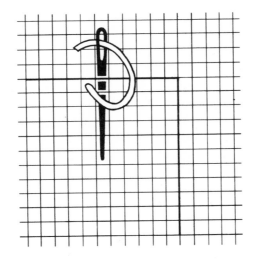

Go back to the beginning of the preceding paragraph and repeat everything it says to do three or four times. Now look back. Stitches are accumulating in a straight forty-five-degree diagonal row that goes from upper left to lower right. The stitches are quite far apart. Keep going until you are one mesh away from the vertical pencil line at the right. Complete the next-to-last stitch; that is, bring the needle and wool through to the front of the canvas. Stop.

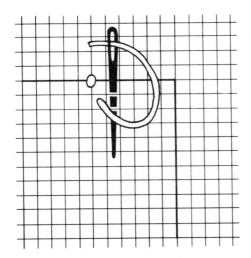
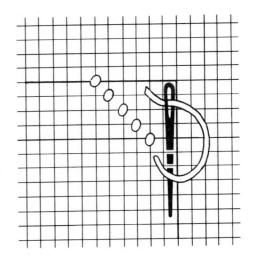

Now you take the last, and odd, stitch of the row, which will get you in position for the second row (it happens to be a Continental stitch taken downward instead of sideways, but don't try to figure this out now.) Do this: Where the wool came up is 1) at the lower left of a pair of crossed threads of canvas. Put the tip of the needle down into 2) the empty space at the upper right of the same crossed threads. Then poke the tip of the needle to the front of the canvas through the empty square space directly *under* 1); that space is 3) for this particular stitch that ends the row. Pull the needle and wool through.

(You need to know that this stitch is made specifically this way to make a straight edge along your pencil line at the right, such as you would make at that edge of a background. In other circumstances, you will start a new, upward row of Basketweave at the point nearest by where the design requires the color of the wool you are using.)

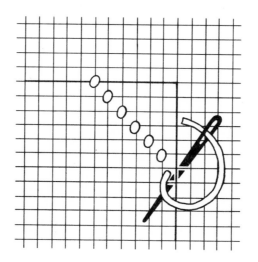

The next row of Basketweave is going to go up instead of down. It will notch in closely to the left of the downward row you have just done. The first move you make will put the needle in the position that defines the second, *horizontal* stage of the Basketweave process.

140

The space where the wool has come up is 1). It is at the lower left of a pair of crossed threads of canvas mesh located directly under the stitch above you just finished. Put the tip of the needle down into the empty square space that is at the upper right 2) of the same pair of crossed threads. Now, in back of the canvas, head the tip of the needle *straight across to the left, horizontally*, under the first vertical mesh of canvas it touches and under the next one to the left as well, then poke the tip of the needle through to the front of the canvas. *Check*: The horizontal needle went into 2); two vertical threads of canvas mesh are lying across it, and these threads are the two sides of a square space the needle has *skipped* (that skipped space is not empty this time; the bottom of the stitch above is in it); and, where the needle came up is 3), an empty square space directly to the left of the skipped one.

(The needle is now in the horizontal stage of the Basket-weave; remember that it is the *needle* that defines this. The *rows* created by this process are the thing that is diagonal.) Pull the needle and wool through.

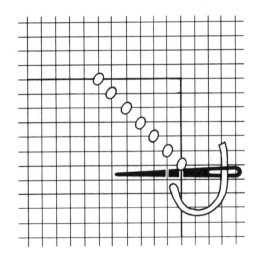

Go back to the beginning of the preceding paragraph and repeat everything it says to do three or four times. Now look back. Stitches are accumulating upward in a forty-five-degree diagonal row that goes from lower right to upper left. The stitches are again quite far apart, but they notch neatly half-

way into the spaces between the stitches of the previous row.
Keep going until you are about to cover the pair of crossed
threads of canvas mesh exactly to the left of the first stitch of
the first row. Stop.

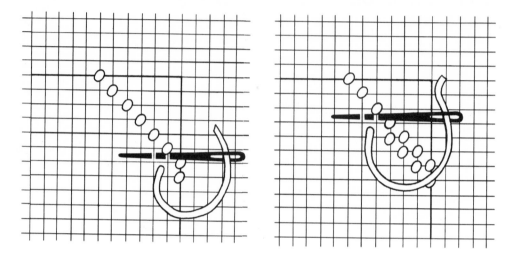

This will be the last, and odd, stitch of the second (upward)
row and will get you in position for the third (downward)
row. Over that pair of crossed threads make a complete Continental stitch; it is not too confusing to say this this time,
because everything is in position to make the Continental stitch
exactly the way you learned it, slanting the needle sideways to
the left.

(Again, you need to know that this Continental stitch is
used specifically to make a straight edge along your top pencil
line, such as you would make at that edge of a background. In
other circumstances, you will start a new, downward row of
Basketweave at the point nearest by where the design requires
the color of the wool you are using.)

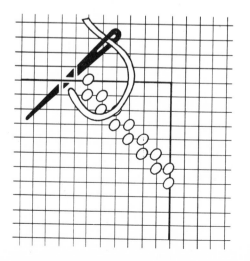

You are ready to start all over again with the last paragraph of instructions on page 138 that defined the *vertical* position of the needle for Basketweave. Keep adding downward and upward rows until you have the feel of how they fit together and how the needle works always straight—either vertically or horizontally—instead of at a slant as it does in the Continental stitch; and, how it always slips under two parallel threads of canvas mesh before coming to the front of the canvas again.

When you get to the knot that first held the wool in place, cut it off. By the time you have gotten that far, it will be clear how the diagonal rows of Basketweave constantly notch into each other; how, even though the stitches are put in in a diagonal sequence, they stack up side by side and up and down along the threads of the canvas mesh to give just the same final effect as the horizontal rows of Continental stitches did. And perhaps it will also be clear that the Basketweave is more fun than the Continental.

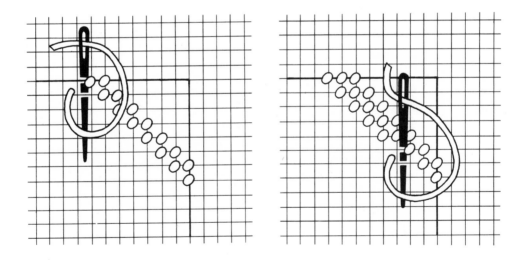

Practicing irregular shapes: This could be helpful. It will remind you of my "makeshift" stitch described earlier (page 134). Draw two small irregular shapes on scraps of canvas. Now fill them in, one with the Continental stitch, the other with the Basketweave. Start stitching, always, at the upper right of the shapes. Immediately something new will show up: You *start* and *end* the rows at unexpected places according to what the outlines of the shapes require. The whole idea of lining up the end stitches to make straight edges goes out the window. Don't let this bother you. Just make sure that each new row—of whichever stitch you are using—is made right next to the last so that *every* pair of crossed threads of canvas mesh gets covered with a lower-left to upper-right stitch. If you understand the stitching, you won't care at all where the design makes you begin and end your rows.

To finish off a strand of wool: In making the last stitch with a piece of wool, take the needle and wool to the back of the canvas and don't bring them forward to the front again. Turn the canvas over, and run needle and wool under the backs of finished stitches for an inch or more. Then cut the wool off quite short.

To begin a new strand of wool: When there is an open area of canvas handy, as in the practice stitching, you can use a knot some distance away from where you are actually stitching which will be cut off later. Or, you can start as you finished in the preceding paragraph: On the back of the canvas, under finished stitches, run the needle from a point an inch or more away to the point where you want to surface to the front and start stitching again.

When you need to skip around with one color: This happens with the "makeshift" stitches, but it happens other times too. When you need more stitches of the same color that you are using in another spot not too far away, it may not be worth the trouble to finish off the strand of wool, cut it off, and restart it in the new spot. Just run the strand under finished stitches at the back of the canvas to the new spot. But do take the trouble to do at least this, because even small "skipping loops" on the back snag and are a nuisance. (You can skip brief distances across the backs of still unstitched areas; later stitches will cover the loop.)

Index

145

How-to Index

148